Writing
Naturally

ALSO BY DAVID PETERSEN

Heartsblood: Hunting, Spirituality, and Wildness in America

Elkheart: A Personal Tribute to Wapiti and Their World

*The Nearby Faraway: A Personal Journey
Through the Heart of the West*

A Hunter's Heart: Honest Essays on Blood Sport (editor)

Ghost Grizzlies: Does the Great Bear Still Haunt Colorado?

*Confessions of a Barbarian: Selections from
the Journals of Edward Abbey* (editor)

Earth Apples: The Poetry of Edward Abbey (editor)

*Racks: The Natural History of Antlers
and the Animals That Wear Them*

Among the Aspen: Life in an Aspen Grove

*Big Sky, Fair Land: The Environmental
Essays of A. B. Guthrie, Jr.* (editor)

Among the Elk: Wilderness Images

Writing Naturally

A Down-to-Earth Guide to Nature Writing

DAVID PETERSEN

Johnson Books
BOULDER

Published by Johnson Books, a division of Johnson Publishing Company, 1880 South 57th Court, Boulder, Colorado 80301.
E-mail: books@jpcolorado.com

9   8   7   6   5   4   3   2   1

Cover design by Debra B. Topping
Cover painting: A detail of "Beaver Dams with a Rising Moon" by
                Thomas Aquinas Daly, from the collection of David
                and Caroline Petersen

Library of Congress Cataloging-in-Publication Data
Petersen, David, 1946–
    Writing naturally : a down-to-Earth guide to nature writing /
    by David Petersen ;
    foreword by H. Emerson Blake.
         p.   cm.
    Includes bibliographical references. (p.).
    ISBN 1-55566-273-0 (alk. paper)
    1. Natural history—Authorship. I. Title.
QH14.P48 2001
808'.066508—dc21   00-054962

Printed in the United States by
Johnson Printing
1880 South 57th Court
Boulder, Colorado 80301

♻ Printed on recycled paper with soy ink

for John Nichols ...
one who walks the talk

Contents

Foreword

NATURE WRITING—good nature writing—requires an openness to the world that is nothing less than extraordinary. It invites the writer on journeys of awe and splendor, but each of those journeys is matched by one that is dark and foreboding. It asks that the writer be willing to confront mystery and complexity head on. It insists that the writer examine every choice he or she makes, and create a philosophy by which to live. Inevitably, it asks the writer to grapple with the messy question of what our place on the planet is.

With prerequisites like these, it's a wonder that anyone even tries writing about nature—it just seems like too much to ask of anyone. Yet there are nature writers everywhere—in cities, suburbs, and countryside, of all ages and creeds and backgrounds—all struggling to come to some new understanding of the natural world and our relationship with it. If you're holding this book, chances are you're one of them.

But writing well about nature requires more than a curiosity about the natural world, and more than a commitment to speak on its behalf. It demands that we master the craft of *writing*—how one uses words to express information and ideas. And for the nature writer, whose writing deals with issues and places and beings that matter so much, the writing must convey much more than information—it must convey feeling. To feel strongly about something is one thing; but to *give* that feeling to another person, and bring that feeling alive in another person's mind and heart, is an entirely different kettle of fish.

The problem with this particular kettle of fish is that many of us who love nature often actually know more about fish than we do about writing. All those outdoor experiences and all that training in natural history are not matched by an equal background in writing. We usually took more courses in science than we did in literature, tend to know more about narwhals than about narrative, and (if you're like me) never totally nailed down the difference between simile and metaphor. Admit it: you would be on surer ground describing what a watershed is, or how birds migrate, than you would explaining allegory or allusion.

This is where David Petersen's *Writing Naturally*—a crash course in the basics of good writing designed expressly for nature writers—comes in.

Oh, but perhaps now you're already resisting. "Simile, schimile," part of you insists, "that stuff is for English majors. I'm not pretending to be an artist." That's a perfectly fine reaction—we who love nature like to believe that our convictions alone will carry our message, and that there's no reason to dress up the message in art. But telling a story *is* an art, and knowing how to tell a story well takes tools, training, and, above all, creative energy and imagination. It is no more realistic to expect someone who had never studied writing to write a powerful, persuasive essay, than it would be to expect someone who had never played the piano to sit down and suddenly make soulful music.

The business of nature itself creates special difficulties for those who write about it, which makes it all the more important that the nature writer have every possible tool at his or her disposal. Any writing that is personal and reflective, which is the case with almost all nature writing, runs the risk of being self-absorbed and narcissistic. Writing that is meant to be celebratory, as is much nature writing, often comes off as being pious, simplistic, and predictable. And testimonies to loss, which unfortunately so much of nature writing must be these days, sound shrill, preachy, and complaining if not expressed correctly. These pitfalls sometimes represent problems of philosophy, as some of nature writing's critics are quick to point out. But more often than not they are problems of writing, and it is through good writing that these problems can be avoided, or transcended. All the better reason for nature writers to hone their skills, gather some tools, and to practice.

Telling a story well takes a lot of practice—there are no shortcuts to becoming a good writer. But it's never a bad idea to have a guide, and David Petersen is as good a guide as you're likely to find. He is, first and foremost, an uncommonly good writer, whose words, says Richard Nelson, are "crisp as a whack with a hard stick." With a dozen books and hundreds of magazine articles to his credit, he is—perhaps more than he would like to be—an authority in the bewildering and sometimes specious world of publishing. He is known among his peers as a writer whose first loyalty is to the truth. In the tradition of his friend Edward Abbey, he has never backed away from the controversial and tough subjects that many writers can't be bothered to tangle with. He is a first-rate naturalist who spends three hundred days a year outdoors. Above all, David is someone who cares as deeply about wildness and wilderness as a person can.

We live in a time in which a wholly new way of thinking about our relationship with the environment is being created. Even if it is not happening at the rate some of us would like, the culture at-large is realizing that our lives are inseparable from the natural world, and that fundamental changes in our relationship with our surroundings have to occur. Nature writers, from Emerson and Thoreau, to Aldo Leopold and Rachel Carson, to today's diverse cadre of essayists, literary journalists, and poets, have played a vital and unique role in shaping new models of how we might live on this planet. They remind us of the wonders—and dangers—surrounding us that so many others have forgotten, or never knew about. They make a difference.

Writing Naturally is a windfall of good ideas and advice for anyone who is striving to make a difference with his or her own nature writing. Whether you are looking to deepen your own appreciation for nature, or to inspire thousands of readers to a new way of thinking, *Writing Naturally* will leave you better prepared for nature writing's challenges, and closer to its rewards.

H. Emerson Blake
Managing Editor
Orion: People and Nature

(A modestly meandering)
Preface

Even reviewers read a preface.
—Philip Guedalla

INDEED THEY DO. Just as savvy newsstand browsers turn straight to the contents page of a magazine to determine quickly if what's inside is worth the price of admission, so do book reviewers often start with the author's preface. This is no put-down; I have been there and so, perhaps, have you. Why is a preface so revealing? Because it's the traditional place to set a book's mood, tone and pace, to establish the author's voice and to preview what's to come, with explanations, excuses and promises as necessary. Perceiving no harm in any of this, I'll comply right now.

By way of self-introduction and to forewarn you "where I'm coming from," I'll begin by stating what I feel to be the one immutably essential qualification to write true, well and accurately about nature: *While I could live without writing, I could never live without the things I write about.*

Those "things," individually and collectively, are wild nature. As the Persian poet Rumi notes: "There are hundreds of ways to kneel and kiss the ground." Having tried a few for myself, I find nature writing—particularly via the personal nature essay—to be the most tasteful.

Why write about nature? *For the love of nature and the writing process*, in that order.

Why *not* write about nature? *For fame and fortune*, neither of which is likely forthcoming in this tragically neglected genre (tragic because the world would be a far better place if more people paid more attention to wild nature) in which the most accessible publication vehicles are nonprofit magazines and small book houses who can't pay much and enjoy only limited distribution and media attention. And all the while, competition increases as more nature writers attempt to shoulder their way into fewer markets. Addressing this latter point—competition—tongue in cheek, novelist (Mary) Flannery O'Connor once quipped: "Everywhere I go, I'm asked if I think the universities stifle writers. My opinion is that they don't stifle enough of them."

Yet, for those who attack it with all the right stuff—including extensive feet-on-the-dirt knowledge of, love for and a passion to learn ever more about wild nature; plus honesty, objectivity, humility, tenacity (and yes, a bit of talent never hurts)—thus armed, there's no other literary genre and few art forms more personally rewarding than nature writing. While other literary genres keep you indoors and draw you inside yourself, making you increasingly anthropocentric, solipsistic and spiritually hidebound, nature writing mandates that you go, regularly and joyfully, *out there*. This mandate, in turn, facilitates philosophical and spiritual growth and offers hope for helping to make this world, *our* world, a better place in which to live and learn.

The living part is utterly up to you. The learning process—learning to see and to *feel* nature and to write meaningfully and movingly about it all—is the subject of this book.

Speaking directly to this point—the individual, artful interpretation of nature for public consumption—American painter and outdoorsman Thomas Aquinas Daly (a sample of whose ethereal work dignifies the cover of this book) says: "I feel that I have just recently begun to develop my own visual language, after many long years of study and practice. Now that I have assimilated a certain amount of academic information and its implementation has become second nature, I feel confident in allowing my intuition a freer rein. I firmly believe that a working knowledge of the basic tools should be established before a painter can successfully embark on a quest for a uniquely personal art. Once the factual material is thoroughly digested, there is an internalized reservoir of reference material to guide more inspired and original modes of expression. Having learned the rules, you then have license to break them, for repeatedly you will find that the reality of painting strays from painting theory."

Indeed it does, just as the reality of living so often strays from political, cultural, liturgical, even legal theory. Ditto for writing. As a full-time professional writer, occasional "literary" book and essay editor and erstwhile writing teacher, I'm convinced that self-tutoring is among the fastest, more enjoyable and overall best ways to learn not only the basic rules of writing, but the creative subtleties of breaking those rules as well.

Admittedly, I do own a degree in creative writing, but such formal education came only after a decade of professional scribbling, editing and self-tutoring, and it furthered my literary progress only insofar as it pointed me in several fresh and unexpected directions for ongoing post-graduate self-edification. Part of the problem, for me, was that back in the ancient days of my protracted college indulgence, at the smallish schools I tended to attend, "creative writing" was largely restricted, in the academic mindset, to poetry and fiction. Nonfiction, being (it was felt) "unimaginative" by comparison, was considered merely utilitarian; something less than creative. Consequently, back then and in my limited experience, the only nonfiction writing classes available were such yawners as composition, semantics and journalism.

Today, formal writing education has markedly improved. Many if not most progressive colleges and universities with viable writing programs now offer classes, even majors, in Essay Writing, Magazine Writing, Creative Nonfiction and Nature Writing. I've taught and even designed a few myself.

All of which is by way of inching toward saying that while studiously *not* following the stuffy style of so many academic writing texts, *Writing Naturally* may nonetheless prove a helpful adjunct to progressive nonfiction writing courses—"nature" and otherwise—from high school to university.

That said, after a quarter-century of professional freelancing, overlain by a dozen years behind a magazine editor's desk (two desks in fact, six years each), a decade of college professing, a few exciting escapades into book editing and occasional workshop teaching, I feel more strongly than ever that informed and purposeful *self*-education is the fastest, surest, certainly the cheapest and withal the *best* way—not merely to learn writing, but to earn publication and recognition as well. Apropos, a primary goal of this book is to facilitate such a personal pursuit.

Yes, a formal writing education *can* help you to write better.

Yes, writing workshops *can* help you to write better.

Yes, how-to books and magazines and even correspondence courses *can* help you to write better.

Yet the best any and all such external aids can do—including the specimen now in hand—is to help you help yourself. What makes good writers isn't nearly so much *teaching* as it is *learning* … learning via reading, studying and dissecting the work of other writers, good and bad; learning by writing and revising and getting rejected and revising some more and weighing informed criticism and eventually getting published and never-ever fooling yourself into believing you know it all. These things, such *self*-directed educational struggles, adapted as a lifestyle, make good writers.

One of the mossiest maxims in writing advises: "Write about what you know." A corollary states that the tandem goals of writing, particularly nonfiction, are to inform and entertain, not necessarily in that order. Both are clichés, granted, yet both are valid, and both are far too frequently ignored. Ernest Hemingway puts it well when he advises writers to "find what gave you the emotion; what the action was that gave you the excitement. Then write it down making it clear so the reader will see it too and have the same feeling that you had."

Or, to trot out yet another helpful cliché: "Show, don't tell."

Long before Hemingway emerged, Goethe said: "He, to whom Nature begins to reveal her open secret, will feel an irresistible yearning for her most worthy interpreter, Art." Similarly, Helen Keller saw the truth clearly when she wrote that "Nature sings her most exquisite songs to those who love her."

The collective point being: You can't write authentically, much less movingly about nature—no matter your writing education and craft level—unless and until you really truly deeply know and *love* nature. And you can't get to know and love nature merely by perusing pretty wildlife magazines or surfing the net for nature sites or sitting in university libraries with your nose in moldy books or watching the Discovery channel. Rather, you must spend every minute you can manage *out there*, in the most natural (wildest) possible environs within ready reach and occasionally far beyond. And often as possible, alone. And while you're out there, you must strive to be an uncommonly keen observer—what Spanish philosopher José Ortega y Gasset, referring specifically to the skilled hunter, calls "the alert man" (even if you're a wo-man).

As Pulitzer-winner Alfred Bertram "Bud" Guthrie, Jr. (*The Big Sky; The Way West*), advises in his crisp little *Field Guide to Writing Fiction* (written when he was ninety):

The combination of personal experience and research opens all doors. The good writer takes the reader on a course of experience. The writer must entertain, else his manuscripts will molder on the shelf, written but unsung. He should also shed at least a ray of light on human experience, on the human condition. These are his moralities, entertainment and illumination, enforced by the high resolve to write his best.

So true, with appropriate elaboration to come. For now, I'll merely repeat that the best nature-writing teacher, beyond nature herself, is *you*, working with and through the four essential elements of literary self-education:

- reading as a writer
- focused writing practice
- tireless revision
- informed, objective criticism

Most of what we'll be discussing across the coming chapters, directly and obliquely, will be aimed at developing, refining and maximizing those four auto-didactic essentials.

A point or two on structure and approach: One element common to academic and "popular" writing manuals that turns readers off like bedroom lights, yet is broadly considered mandatory, is the "Practice Exercise" section, trailing each chapter like body odor. With rare exceptions, these "homework" requirements seem impractical (at least in "popular" writing books, with no instructor physically present to coerce participation and constructively criticize student efforts) and a big fat boor to boot.

Yet, on-point exercises can help greatly to clarify, reinforce and personalize information presented in the text. Therefore, by way of felicitous compromise and to remove the toothless bite of "mandatory" from the equation, let's render our practice exercises optional, for me as well as for you. When clearly useful drills come to mind, I'll suggest them. When they don't, I won't. You can take or leave them as you choose, and feel free to invent your own. No guilt implied or necessary, on either side of the page.

What else? Well, there's the sticky wicket of examples. At first look, the almost universal tendency of authors of popular writing manuals to "carry on" about their own trials and accomplishments as writers, and to offer copious excerpts from their own work to exemplify points they're trying to make—such "Hey, look at *me* kids!" tactics seem overtly egoistic. And often they are. Yet on closer inspection there are practical justifications for such seeming self-indulgence. Such as: No writer can know or explain the stylistic intent of another writer's work nearly so clearly, accurately and authoritatively as she or he who actually wrote it. A. B. Guthrie summarizes this fix in his own prefatory caveat to his own writing book: "If on occasion I use lines from my own work as illustrations, it is not because they are superior, but because they are mine and ready to hand." My sentiment and predicament exactly. However, I'm acutely aware of the dangers and as often as possible will employ as examples the work of other, better, writers.

Which brings us to the related concern of "favorites." A majority of the illustrative and inspirational quotes in *Writing Naturally* come from male writers—including such "macho" and "sexist" characters as Ernest Hemingway and Edward Abbey, opening me to charges of gender bias. Frankly, this is neither my intent nor my concern. My intent and concern are helping hopeful writers become published writers, and published writers become better. In that quest I must employ the most telling examples that I know. No slight or sexism intended.

Finally, in addition to the "normal" chapters, you'll find "Instructive Interludes" planted like mines throughout the text. Each is intended not only to exemplify and clarify issues discussed in preceding chapters—most often *the* preceding chapter—but to add a little something new, and a bit more personal, to the stew.

And that, as "they" say, is that.

Let's all just relax and try to have some fun with what's to come. At the least, I can assure you that *Writing Naturally* will be different. (Which is not, you'll note, a value judgment.)

A lifetime ago, an aging Aldo Leopold looked around and allowed as how he wouldn't care to be young again without wild country to be young in.

Me too. How about you? How about our kids and theirs? And what can we, mere humble scriveners, *do* about it?

In cumulative fact, quite a lot: *Words make a difference.*

Acknowledgments

"NATURE WRITER." When called one, Ed Abbey was wont to retort: "What the hell is *that?*"

Whatever it is, its definition is necessarily bifurcate, comprising two separate things—nature and writing—each having, in my life, appropriately separate influences. In the writing arena, and regarding specifically this little book, I'm acutely thankful to my co-conspirators Stephen Topping (editor most amiable and able), Mira Perrizo, Stephanie White, Richard Croog and the other fine folk at Johnson Books for taking me on yet again. (Slow learners, that bunch.) John Murray, a long-time friend, positively influenced these pages. I'm deeply honored to have a detail from the numinous "Beaver Ponds with Rising Moon," by the great American watercolorist Thomas Aquinas Daly, adorning the cover of this book. And working artfully with and around Daly's art, Debra B. Topping's cover design is simply elegant.

English Professor emeritus Mark Coburn and I conspired years ago to write "A College Writing Short-Course" for a writer's magazine. With Mark's permission, that piece is reborn here.

The foreword, by *Orion* magazine's illustrious and industrious managing editor, H. Emerson "Chip" Blake, is informed, eloquent and generous, for all of which I am humbly grateful. Chip also read the manuscript in progress and offered invaluable comments, as did my dear friend Florence Rose Shepard, my favorite daughter Christine Petersen and my live-in managing editor, Caroline Petersen. I thank you for your courage and support, all and one.

Throughout the years I spent teaching writing, I was told often by students that my approach was somehow "different" and I therefore should collect my class notes into a book. But

I never did. Then, in the summer of 1998, I was invited to teach a nature writing seminar at the Yellowstone Institute, for which occasion I updated, expanded and reorganized my copious college notes for the less formal, more relaxed and compressed institute setting—and there again, I was openly urged to write a book about writing. So this time I did. Were it not for that Yellowstone experience and encouragement, I don't know if I would ever have overcome my dis-ease with the idea of writing about writing—which act, after all, implies you think you know what the hell you're talking about. So, if you don't think I know what the hell I'm talking about, please feel free to blame it all on the overly enthusiastic participants in the 1998 Yellowstone Institute nature writing workshop. (You know who you are, and so do I.)

Shifting now to the realm of nature-love and nature-knowledge, my primary professors have been hunting, hiking, fishing, camping, wild landscapes, wild wapiti and grizzly bears, the Boy Scouts, Edward Abbey, Tom Beck, Paul Shepard, instinct, instinctive iconoclasm and the great good luck to have been born and raised in a time and place where nature could still be found and freely enjoyed just a bicycle ride from home. As students of human ecology have so well documented, and our increasingly virtual culture so blithely ignores, a childhood deprived of nature leaves one hell of a hole to pull yourself out of.

I also love my dogs, Otis and Willie.

For all of these and all of this, and for you, indulgent reader, I thank my lucky stars.

These things can be told. But there are no words that can tell of the hidden spirit of the wilderness, that can reveal its mystery, its melancholy and its charm.

—Theodore Roosevelt, *African Game Trails*

CHAPTER 1

The Nature
of Nature Writing

*Of human utterances there are two types: those that are forgotten
and those that are remembered. Those that are remembered are
notable, so we can say that literature is notable utterances.*

—Gary Snyder

A GOOD AND PROPER PLACE to begin is with the question:
What *is* "nature writing"? One way to approach a meaningful
answer is to explore what nature writing is *not*.

A kindred, confusing and often confused term is "natural
history." To be pedantically precise, natural history is a close
sister to nature writing and a significant ingredient, among
many, of personal nature narrative. In the words of Edward O.
Wilson (*Biophilia*): "The special role of natural history writing is to incorporate the best of science in order to re-examine
the natural world and the humanities' place within it in the
scientific mode but through the prisms of literary expression."

Toward that end, pure natural history focuses on exposition—a teaching technique we'll look at more closely in the
next chapter, but which we can simply say, for now, equates to
"explanation." Pure natural history generally restricts itself to
enumerating, describing, categorizing, interpreting and otherwise explaining the elements and workings of the natural
world—and, at the best of times, doing so with grace and style,
"through the prisms of literary expression." While generally

written in the third-person (impersonal: "she, he, they") voice, natural history can be otherwise—and that's where distinctions dim, to the degree that a great many writers, editors, educators and reviewers have come to view and use the terms "nature writing" and "natural history" interchangeably.

Right or wrong, I do not.

To my eyes, ears and sensibilities, true nature writing is far more than explicative natural history, no matter how prettily put. It is overtly concerned with compositional *creativity*, paying close heed to such expressive elements as style (also called "voice"), character development, point of view, vocabulary, even—as exemplified and personified by Edward Abbey, Terry Tempest Williams and others—word-playfulness, plus forceful opinion and open criticism of the antinature status quo in our and other cultures. Additionally and in sum, nature writing strives to be literate (well-written and of lasting value) and most often is not only first-person but intimately personal.

Lately, mostly in academic circles, rustic old nature writing has been granted a titular promotion to "environmental literature." All good intent aside, this grandiose moniker is both overly restrictive and misleading, implying that nature writing is roped tightly to environmental issues, and thus primarily polemical in tone and political in thrust. Not so. As with natural history, environmentalism often is an *element* of nature writing, but never the whole shebang and no way mandatory. Environmental writing is "something else again."

But if it's neither "natural history" nor "environmental literature," what *is* this thing called "nature writing?"

By my lights, it's any nonfiction prose that has as its central theme—be it face-slapping overt or subtly so—a celebration of *wild* nature (as opposed to domestic, pastoral, bucolic or otherwise tamed and man-ipulated virtual nature). Further, true nature writing is intended and intoned for popular consumption. Moreover (and again), nature writing strives to be "literary"—which doesn't mean formal or fancy, but merely serious, thoughtful, informed, personal, artful and of tenacious merit.

Which brings us to yet another important and confusing distinction. "The difference between literature and journalism," quipped Oscar Wilde, "is that journalism is unreadable and literature is not read." As sadly true as that statement may be—statistically at least—it's a non sequitur in our genre in that we, as nature writers, knowingly commit ourselves to producing a "product" that relatively few Americans will ever read. But ah! Those few! Those brave and loyal few! How they depend on and appreciate us—even as we need and do love them. Thus, onward, unto the breach and back on topic.

The differences (between journalism and lit) are many, though one is primary: the presence or absence of the writer on the page. A foundation tenet of journalism, especially news journalism, is that the writer remain invisible and opinionless—a mechanistic reporter of facts and, at most, other people's opinions. In pointed contrast, narrative nonfiction is necessarily first-person and profoundly invested with (colored by) the writer's personality, including especially opinion. Virtually all journalism—excepting Hunter Thompson-style "gonzo" journalism, which isn't journalism at all but a subtle, sophisticated and delightfully profane expression of intellectual iconoclasm as literary art—except for this, most journalism is written in third person, past tense. By contrast, creative nonfictive literature, nature and otherwise, is most often first-person but freely employs third- and even second-person, as well as all three tenses, mixed and matched at will.

Certainly, there's the viable in-between of "literary" journalism, which strives to accomplish the goals of both without the gonzo punch of "new" journalism. Yet, as put by one of the leading writers in our genre, Barry Lopez (*Arctic Dreams*), nature writing is more, in that it strives to provide "an antidote to solipsism." It's "not just about polar bears, or some other kind of animal, or plants or birds. It's about the fundamental issues of life. [Nature writers] reach across some dangerous chasm, where they are at great risk, to inquire of a parallel culture, to ponder another order, for how it might illuminate some part of their own culture."

Indeed—an honestly emotional human nature/wild nature connection is *mandatory* to successful, meaningful, lasting nature writing. All of the best—most thought-provoking and readable—nature writers are avid campfire philosophers.

Beyond such basic distinctions, the horizons grow foggy. For instance, can fiction qualify as nature writing? Insofar as the human/nature connection is explicated and celebrated, you bet it can. Yet fiction is fabrication and nonfiction is fact—a critical distinction to be pricked, poked and explored somewhere farther along. For now, for our present purpose, let's consider fidelity to reality a requisite to the sort of "nature writing" under discussion.

Likewise, can popular (that is, mass-market) science writing qualify as nature writing? Hard to say. Take, for a celebrated example of the pop-science genre, Stephen Jay Gould, who's written several books as well as a long-running column for *Natural History* magazine. Gould is a wonderful academic explicator, striving always to minimize gratuitous esoteric jargon, keeping his message accessible, warmly personal, light and even lightly humorous. Yet, because he and most other pop-science writers intend primarily to explicate and entertain—rather than to place humanity (back) in an appropriate context with wild nature—I argue that science writing, even the best pop-science writing, is not true nature writing. Nor need it be; remember, we're not ranking here, but merely differentiating.

And speaking of "rank," what about so-called *outdoor* writing, a term most often used in reference to lowly "hook-and-bullet" (fishing and hunting) journalism but also encompassing other areas of outdoor recreation, such as wilderness travel and adventure? Can this be nature writing? Again, as with pop-science, it *can* be, but rarely is. Certainly, the bulk of hook-and-bullet is fly-blown carrion at worst and mildly informative journalism at best (a handful of platinum exceptions gratefully noted, such as *Fly Rod & Reel's* Ted Williams and Canada's Kevin Van Tighem), focusing on how-to, where-to, "Me and Joe" divertissement and gadget flacking, with little or no appreciation for, or understanding of, the living landscape surrounding the action nor even the creatures that action is aimed at, much less the vital human/nature connection.

Yet hunting helped to make us human (for satisfyingly scientific and philosophical verification of this outrageous claim, see Paul Shepard's *The Tender Carnivore and the Sacred Game*). Moreover, this ancient, essentially honorable activity, when undertaken in the right (neo-animistic) spirit, continues to connect humanity in deeply personal, meaningful and ecologically positive ways with wild nature—the way, you could say, "God planned it"—rather than merely observing from the sidelines as inert, impotent and detached spectators. Not surprisingly, a significant number of the most informed, feeling and convincing nature writers, past and present, were introduced to nature through "filthy blood sport." Consider J. J. Audubon, Aldo Leopold, Ernest Thompson Seton, Theodore Roosevelt, Peter Matthiessen (who once captained a deep-sea sport-fishing boat), Richard Nelson (a subsistence deer slayer), Paul Shepard, John Nichols—the list is long and exceedingly dignified.

So yes, hook-and-bullet journalism *can be* nature writing—or, more often, include aspects and elements of nature writing—although it rarely is or does. Ditto wilderness travel writing that focuses on such silent, low-impact, muscle-powered locomotion as backpacking and canoeing—depending, again, on the writer's attention to the wild/human synergy, style of delivery, intellect, intent and personality.

But returning now to "pure" nature writing, as committed by Henry Thoreau, Richard Nelson, Ann Zwinger, Robert Michael Pyle, John Nichols and Edward Abbey (though the latter steadfastly denied it, preferring, tongue wagging in cheek, to be called "a creator of fine fictions and elegant essays"), Terry Tempest Williams and dozens more. This is the genuine article, the true good stuff, the genre and quality I aspire to and hope to inspire you to: the bullseye we'll be shooting for in the discussions, readings and exercises to follow. And it all—nature writing—shares one common element, as noted by the patriarch of western American literature (and former editor of the journal by that name), Thomas J. Lyon (*This Incomparable Land*): "A distinguishing mark of the nature essay—and this has been true from the beginnings of the genre onward—is precisely the attempt to harmonize *fact* knowledge and *emotional* knowledge [thus gaining] the wholeness of outlook that characterizes the best nature writing."

"Wholeness of outlook." *That's* the ticket.

It's often said that Henry David Thoreau, working in the mid-1800s, was the world's first nature writer. I think not. What Thoreau was, was the first American nature writer to achieve world recognition. He essentially invented the personal nature essay, so popular today, and was and remains, thus, the single greatest influence on many of the best nature writers to follow. And to come.

Yet, giving equal time to that old devil criticism, many contemporary readers find Henry's prose a hard row to hoe and woefully "out of style" today. While we love such pithy and tenacious Thoreauvian epigrams as "In wildness is the preservation of the world" and "All good things are wild and free," his style is oft-times so elaborately convoluted, his vocabulary so extravagant and his cultural context so antiquated, that he can be fully appreciated only by neo-transcendentalists, college lit professors and other intellectual masochists.

Still, Henry set the pace, lit the way and fairly defined American nature writing by being the first to blend extensive field observation, careful research, a passionately personal voice brimming with independence, iconoclasm, opinion, humanity, emotion, truth and wit, with an authentic and penetrating love for the natural world—all delivered in an artfully original voice, including especially the skillfully creative use of figurative language. How can such as *that* ever go "out of style"?

It cannot. All of the best nature writers today evidence subtle Thoreauvian influences in their work, aware of it or no, and notwithstanding that many—Abbey, who both praised and pilloried Thoreau, is a delightful example—could hardly be less like Henry in personality, voice and lifestyle. While Thoreau strikes most ears as Ivy League elite, Abbey's voice is that of an eloquent redneck; a real and regular guy with a healthy sense of humor and an even healthier libido. (Two essentials of the good life that Henry sorely lacked—laughter and lust—abetting, perhaps, his premature demise.)

Which brings us—unavoidably, if several chapters before its time—to a preview of the topic of "voice." We'll talk a lot about voice and style before we're out of these wordy woods, but since we're here, I feel compelled to comment that if you're struggling to develop a literary style of your own, you could do worse than to begin with a relaxed, conversational, *natural* voice. *Your* voice. Don't try, as some have done and do, to sound like Thoreau. Nor like Abbey. "Both of them fellers is dead." And both aped themselves far better than you or I ever could. Rather, learn what you can from the old masters, but strive always and ever for originality. Relax. Don't take your writing, or yourself, too seriously. And *never* try to fake your knowledge of, or love for, nature.

Consider, on this topic, the following all-too-common and still-growing criticisms of contemporary nature writing and writers, lodged by frustrated magazine editors, book reviewers and nature writers themselves:

> The trouble with most nature writing is that it's always reaching, trying to tease great thoughts, great metaphors, out of the world. It's a kind of narcissism, an ego on parade: "Look how well I can write, Mom." (*Men's Journal*)

> Writing well about the experience of being in the wild lands of the West is a remarkable feat. These days everyone wants to do it, but most of the stories we hear are told from the outside looking in. I have grown weary of seeing new books sensationalizing the creatures and habitats that lure so many out West. [Few writers] can make it crystal clear that there is terrible loss occurring in the natural world without sounding like fingernails on chalkboard. (*Northern Lights*)

> Despite the current popularity of "nature writing," it seems only a few authors can make it palatable, and even fewer seem willing to give natural history the deeper context, perspective and reflection needed to make it relevant. (*Inside/Outside Southwest*)

> Recently I gave up on trying to read a famous nature writer's latest work after encountering the pronoun "I" eighteen times on the first page. The writer appeared lonely, self-centered and smug all at the same time. (*Writers on the Range*, a syndicated service of *High Country News*)

The lessons and cautions implied in such complaints are manifold: Don't consciously affect either a professorial or a "pretty" voice; don't get preachy or adopt an unrelenting Chicken Little doomsday tone; don't try to fake experience or force external meaning onto nature; keep the focus on your topic rather than yourself and, above all, *know your subject intimately* and in explicating and defending it, don't shy away from controversy or criticism.

In sum, too much nature writing today is experientially uninformed, thus viscerally detached, sentimental and smarmy.

"Far too many of those who write about nature," complains Pulitzer poet Gary Snyder, "have no experience whatsoever of what they write. They have never actually seen the glint in the eye of an eagle or the way a lizard's ribs quake when he does push-ups, or the way a trout turns and flicks, or how a bear backs up. If you haven't seen these things you shouldn't write about them … if it is inauthentic it will show up sooner or later."

To write well—believably and meaningfully—about wild nature and our relationship to it, there's no way around indulging in an orgy of personal experience *in* wild nature. Which is *not* to suggest that you go out and "do" nature in order to have something to write about—such forced association shows, and it's rarely very pretty. Rather, write to share your spontaneous experiences in and feelings for wild nature with others—experiences and feelings you'd seek, from deep personal need, even if you weren't a writer.

While I could live without writing, I could never live without the things I write about.

Well said, if I do say so myself.

Optional exercise

Make lists of what you do and don't like about the styles of various nature writers—the living, the dead, the living-dead— then expand those lists into a critical essay of comparison, contrast and personal comment.

The point: To provide practice in thinking and writing critically about writing, to help clarify what *you* consider the essential elements, parameters and goals of "nature writing" and—most important—to help identify and internalize what does and does not work for you stylistically, and why. Having done so, next time you sit down to write you'll have a better idea, consciously or subconsciously, of where you want to go, how best to get there and why.

Knee-Deep in Its Absence

OCCASIONALLY, I'M ASKED why I've chosen to make my career (so-called) writing about nature. The answer is easy: I *have* no choice; it's in my genes, and in my heart. As it just may be in yours.

The best scientific guess is that crude, "proto" language first appeared among the progenitors of our species more than two million years ago. Full, "true" language, it is thought, evolved no earlier than one hundred thousand and no later than forty thousand years ago, exactly in synch with the triumphant emergence of *Homo sapiens sapiens*. (Coincidental? Not likely. The ability to communicate intricate thoughts no doubt gave early *H. s. sap* a survival edge over his less eloquent contemporary, *H. s. neandertalensis;* and in evolutionary competition between two species competing for the same niche, any edge is—well, an edge.)

At that time and until the most recent moment of human history, our hunter-gatherer ancestors had no cultivated crops, no domesticated livestock, no industry beyond local, small-scale production of artful implements of stone, bone (including antler and horn), wood and natural fibers. And since we also had no writing, all accumulated knowledge— social and religious values, tribal and family histories, myth, law, legend, ritual, *everything*—had to be precisely memorized and orally transmitted from generation to generation. And what better vehicle for organizing, condensing, memorizing and transferring the spoken word, than—story.

Which is to say: For the overwhelming bulk of human history on this lovely Earth, *our* nature was inseparable from wild nature; we *were* wild nature. It follows naturally that the characters who breathed life into ancestral story would have taken, and in surviving primitive cultures continue to take, the form of animals, animal-humans, animal-gods, even (as in Navajo creation myth) animated landscapes.

Only about ten thousand years ago did we begin to tame wild flora and fauna, gradually trading spear, atlatl and digging stick for plow and shepherd's crook, thus initiating our self-eviction from the Eden of pristine nature. In due time came industry, that irresistible magnet for urban growth. Thus, only in the last micro-second of human history has so-called progress insidiously separated the majority of humanity from daily association first with wild, then pastoral nature. Simultaneous with and due to this estrangement, the ancestral literature of nature and place, which had thrived for countless millennia, began to fall out of use, out of favor, being replaced first in oral tradition, then—beginning some thirty-five hundred years ago with the invention of the first complex alphabets—in written literature. Thus, with "progress" came a transition from the oral literature of wild nature to story increasingly focused on an increasingly human-constructed world. In the second half of the fifteenth century, Gutenberg's printing press appeared, facilitating and speeding that sad transmogrification, so evident in the King James Bible.

But all that riseth returneth to Earth, and now, in this living generation, as we witness the last remnants of wild nature being clear-cut, bulldozed, blacktopped and otherwise "improved" into extinction, as the spiritual quality of our lives atrophies while our material "standard of living" continues to bloat, nature-story is recapturing its deeply historical popularity and significance. At least so among literate, thinking readers, who feel what may well be a genetic craving for nature-based story; story that reconnects us to our ancestral roots and rejoins us, at least in spirit, with the natural world that was and is our only home; story which, like any useful religion, gives direction and meaning to our un-naturally complex lives and offers hope for the future by embracing values from our formative past.

Naturally, the character of the place in which a nature writer lives and works (or longs to return to) colors his or her work. For Wendell Berry it's rural Kentucky. For Terry Tempest Williams the Great Basin and Colorado Plateau. For Richard Nelson it's coastal Alaska. For Ann Zwinger and Edward Abbey the entire Southwest. For A. B. Guthrie, Jr. the Big Sky country of Montana. For John Nichols the *Milagro* country in and around the Taos Valley.

My own place is the San Juan Mountains of southwestern Colorado. I thrive on the crisp clean air and cold clear water here, the breath-sucking beauty of the creased and crenulated landscape and its abundant wildlife, the relative quiet and solitude and the personal joy it all adds up to. *These* are the things I have come to value most in life. It follows that these are also the things I am compelled to write about. In my case at least, the nature of the place has become the nature of the man, of the writer.

During the first few years that Caroline and I lived here, high in the southern Rockies, we had a most pleasant habit of walking or snow-shoeing a mile down the mountain to spend Sunday mornings lazing around an antique woodstove drinking coffee and chatting with an octogenarian rancher friend named Helen. Having spent her entire long life on the verdant riverside spread where she was born in 1905, Helen is

living local history and a captivating storyteller. Among my
favorites is her tale of the naked fat man.

In the summer of 1913, when Helen had just turned eight,
her father went hunting up the tight little creek valley where
my hillside cabin now squats. There, "in blow-down timber so
thick you couldn't ride a horse through," Helen's father killed
an exceptionally large, brown-colored bear that could have
been the dead-last grizzly in these parts. With helping hands
and horses, the hunter hauled the bruin home and hoisted it
by the hind legs into a sturdy tree, then skinned it in preparation for butchering. (Few country folk in those lean and
pragmatic days wasted fresh meat of any kind, and "woods
pork" was widely considered a delicacy.)

It was then, with the bare bear hanging there and her father
standing beside it, bloody knife in hand, that young Helen
wandered into the scene. Horrified at what she saw, she burst
into tears and fled. Eighty years later, Helen laughs when she
recalls how that poor flayed bear "looked like a naked fat man
hanging there. I thought Dad had killed somebody and was
fixing to cut him up and feed him to us. I haven't been able to
stomach bear meat since."

Story spawns story.

Some years ago, while exploring a secluded aspen grove some
miles up the mountain from my cabin, I stumbled upon a hidden spring. Abundant spoor announced that deer, elk, bears,
turkeys and other wildlife visited the place regularly to drink
from the little pool, to browse the lush vegetation watered by
the pool's brief overflow and, I like to think, just to be there.

Shadowy and quiet and just a bit spooky at twilight, the
place exudes a preternatural ambience. Since that day I've
visited this sylvan shrine often; it has become my local refuge
from Babylon. And among the most significant elements of
the spirit of the place are its bear trees: Across the decades,

the soft white skins of several of the larger aspens ringing the spring have collected hundreds of blackened bear-claw scars. This in itself is hardly unique. I've seen scores of bruin-scarred aspens near dozens of secluded spring pools throughout the Rockies. Most often, it's black bear cubs that do the climbing and whose needle-sharp claws scratch and gouge the impressionable bark, leaving distinctively curved, parallel signatures. As the aspens grow, these modest tracks harden, blacken, stretch and swell, eventually coming to look as if they were made by the most monstrous of bruins.

But two special aspens near my spring wear a different sort of signature entirely: heavy, widely spaced vertical claw marks more than a foot long and at just the right height, allowing for decades of subsequent growth, to suggest that a very large bear once stood upright, stretched as high as possible and raked heavily downward—exactly as grizzlies are wont to do.

In parallel with my old friend Helen, those storybook aspens have survived nearly a century rooted firmly in this cloistered San Juan pocket. I find it a deeply poignant experience to sit quietly in that enchanted refugium and study those crude autographs and imagine them being inscribed by Helen's "naked fat man" himself. Not likely, of course. But possible nonetheless.

On one of the last occasions Caroline and I went to visit Helen, I found myself admitting to her that I was terribly envious of the simple, self-sufficient, quietly satisfying life she'd known while growing up and living on a working ranch in the good old days of a still-wild West. "I'd give anything," I confessed, "to have lived your life."

"Hell," Helen snorted, "you can *have* my life. I wish I'd been born fifty years sooner." Surprised, I asked why.

"So I wouldn't be around today to see what the sons-abitches are doing to this place."

What the Buddha Might Say, Were She Here Today
    In the forest
    walk, sit, see.
    Inhale ... silence.
    Exhale ... solace.
    At the forest's edge
    live
    gently
    without pretense or harm.

As another old friend, A. B. Guthrie Jr., was quick to warn: "The thing you've got to watch out for with 'progress' is, there's no turning back."

Helen is pushing one hundred now and no longer guides hunters and fly fishers on wilderness horse-packing trips or plants a big garden or keeps chickens by the score or hauls hay out to feed snow-stranded cattle or drives a horse-drawn sleigh fourteen miles to town for medicine in winter blizzards. No more grizzlies in the neighborhood either.

Instead, we have ever more care-less destroyers. Ever more new roads slicing like daggers into the shrinking heart of wildness. Ever more urban refugees arriving to build ever more pretentious, wasteful houses along those new roads. My magical bear trees are in mortal danger of being "harvested" for the polluting pulp mill that makes the waferboard used to build those houses. Wal-Mart is upon us.

"The thought of what was here once and is gone forever will not leave me as long as I live. It is as though I walk knee-deep in its absence."

Wendell Berry said that, and I live it with him daily.

Standard advice to aspiring writers is: "Write about what you know about." For aspiring nature writers, I'd refine that to: Write about what you know about and *love*.

CHAPTER 2

The Essay

Fitting Form to Function

Thoreau had been walking along the stony shore of Walden Pond on a cool and cloudy summer evening when, for no particular reason that he could single out, the "environment," as we call it, and the "self," as we call it, became numinously coparticipant: "Sympathy with the fluttering alder and poplar leaves almost takes away my breath ..." This is the lyric core of the nature essay. It is the experienceable aspect of ecology. —Thomas J. Lyon

WAXING COMMERCIAL for a moment (about as long, my wife and agent will affirm, as I'm capable of being commercial):

The two primary print outlets for nature writing are *periodicals*—comprising magazines, journals and, occasionally, newspaper editorial and "weekend magazine" sections—and *books*. And often as not, nature books are—overtly or covertly—mere collections (anthologies) of nature essays. Most of the essays in David Quammen's award-winning *Natural Acts* were written originally for his long-running *Outside* magazine column of the same name. Jim Harrison, Peter Matthiessen, John Nichols, Ann Zwinger and countless others have done the same.

Of the eight books I've written (the others I merely edited), two of my own favorites (*Elkheart* and *The Nearby Faraway*) are collections of a score or so essays each, most of which saw first print in magazines and are but loosely related in theme, arranged to present some semblance of cohesion. By contrast, *Ghost Grizzlies* and *Heartsblood* are almost wholly original and were written according to an overarching plan. In fact, *Heartsblood* is *so* tightly knit that I find it frustratingly difficult to do a public reading of any one chapter, or section thereof, without feeling woefully out of context. (Lesson: Always include at least one "stand alone" chapter for public readings.) Yet even those two "planned" books contain bits recycled from magazine essays.

All of which is by way of proposing that the essay is the primary, most useful and potentially most artful expression of personal nature narrative—always has been, always will be. Furthermore, if you can write good essays you can write good books, since structurally, chapters are to books as paragraphs are to essays. Consequently, the personal essay is a form all serious nature writers must first comprehend as readers, then strive to make their own.

Which prompts the pertinent query: What *is* an "essay," nature or otherwise?

According to my wayworn *Arcade Dictionary of Word Origins*, both *essay* and *assay* trace back to a common Latin root infinitive—*exagium*, "to weigh." In Old French we see a transition to *assaier*, meaning "to test." In modern French the noun form *Essais* first sees light as the title of Montaigne's 1580 collection of "short nonfictional literary compositions." Knowing a good idea when he stole one, Francis Bacon gave his own (1597) nonfiction collection the title *Essays*, establishing the word, along with its spelling and literary meaning, in modern English.

By combining the ancient "to weigh"—or, more broadly, according to *Webster's 10th*, "trial, test, effort, attempt"—with "a short nonfictional literary composition," we're finally getting somewhere. Again according to *Webster's*, an essay is "an analytic or interpretative literary composition usually dealing with its subject from a limited or personal point of view."

And so it is that Sam Johnson nailed it dead-on when he defined the literary essay as "a rambling disquisition on a limited theme." Or, as Herman Melville notes in "that big fish story": "There are some enterprises in which a careful disorderliness is the true method."

Indeed, it's the essay's carefully disordered, rambling and personable flavor that makes the form so very attractive, to reader and writer alike. In fact, you can visualize and even plot the structure and progress of an essay with the mnemonic: "Ramble and return." While an essay, by definition, wanders hither and yon, each and every ramble necessarily returns to connect, if only briefly and discreetly, with the spinal theme— the premise being explored, weighed, meditated, masticated and artfully circumambulated—before wandering off in some fresh direction. And with each exploratory ramble and return, the theme is somehow furthered toward its conclusion.

Thus—simmering all the foregoing down to the specific instance under consideration—we can fairly define the contemporary nature essay as the literary treatment of a limited subject from a limited and personal point of view, employing an unlimited variety of approaches and techniques to render the whole not only informative and convincing, but entertaining and inspiring if not downright epiphanous.

But etymology, spelling and definition aside, the important thing to know and remember—and to bear out in your writing—is that the essay should be fun to read and fun to write, even when its theme is woefully serious. (Sound impossible? Read Abbey, Terry Williams, or John Nichols.) That said, let's move beyond external form and plunge into the guts of the thing.

The personal nature essay can be any length, so long as it doesn't belie the bounds of "short" (a rough norm is two- to five-thousand words), and so long as every syllable earns its slot. Be careful not to gnaw off too much, as too broad a topic will force you into superficiality—nor too little, as too narrow a focus begs filler and fluff. Shoot for a thorough, detailed, yet tenably *limited* discussion of a *limited* topic, painted as concisely as possible without making the reader feel cramped. Generally and within reason, shorter is better, especially regarding your chances for publication. The most sublime of essays, with every phrase measured, weighed and layered in meaning, fly under the flag of poetry.

Unlike journalism, scholarly writing and most natural history, the essay uses the personal voice (first-person: I, me, my) and employs a complex plethora of creative ingredients traditionally associated with fiction—including figurative language, some form or shadow of a plot, plus place-setting, clever manipulation of tense and person, character development, foreshadowing, flashback, immediacy and more.

Overall, the essay style you're shooting for is natural and conversational—which can be anything from (unpretentiously) sophisticated to creatively casual, so long as it remains compelling throughout and isn't stiff, arrogant, boring, solipsistic or just too cute. Like a pilot in flight, you want to keep your vehicle trim and clean of all unnecessary appendages in an effort to minimize drag. Specifically, such awkward academic appurtenances as footnotes and textual citations have no place in the personal essay or narrative-driven nature book. A recent and sterling example of one writer's creativity in meeting the challenge of having her cake and devouring it too, regarding extensive footnotes, is Terry Tempest Williams's mystical garden of artful delights, *Leap*. While the main text—comprising four extended, courageously experimental essays—is footnote-free; the final fifth of the book consists of hundreds of notes, arranged by chapter and page and keyed to the text by repeating, in boldface type, the opening sentence or phrase of the section to which each note refers. Once you get with the program, it's easy to use, even fun, and a whole lot cleaner than footnotes.

Among the most lucrative exercises for coming to intimate terms with the narrative nature essay—comprehending and conquering the beautiful beast—is to study the published work of other writers; dissecting the whole to find its spine and ribs, examining each rib in turn for its role in moving the theme, premise, goal, toward a satisfying—not necessarily profound; merely satisfying is fine—conclusion.

Once again: Essay writing involves the artful assemblage and movement of seemingly disparate parts toward a unified end. And toward that end, the calculated rambles can and generally do embrace a wide, even wild, variety of elements and approaches, not uncommonly including:

- Quotes, from conversation as well as print
- Pertinent facts, including statistics
- History
- Personal observation, leading to logically induced or deduced speculation and prediction (hypothesis)
- Dialogue (snippets of conversation)
- Internal monologue ("thinking out loud")
- Provocative queries ("But what if ...?")
- Humor
- Anecdote (a brief, self-contained story with a point, often but not always told in first-person: "I'm reminded of the time when my fishing buddy George ...").

That's a start; those parts. Yet more is/are needed. In order to deconstruct (in reading) or construct (in writing) an essay, identify its bits and determine how each contributes (or not) to the whole, and in order to see how, and how effectively, all those bits come together, puzzlelike, to form a focused picture, we need some universal concepts, elements and nomenclature to hang our thoughts on.

There are four basic kinds—types, species, categories—of nonfiction writing, each comprising a happily unpredictable slumgullion of the ingredients listed above and, of course, "more." While a working familiarity with this categorical quorum won't in itself make you a better writer (well, maybe just a little bit), it *will* facilitate an informed analysis of the techniques employed by other writers, and yourself, along with their relative effectiveness. These four categories, or basic essay components, are:

- Description
- Exposition
- Argumentation
- Narration

Since a memorable mnemonic here is the acronym DEAN (as in James, Jimmy or university), we'll discuss them in that order, though it really doesn't matter, as they're sympatric, synergetic elements of the selfsame whole; a compositional ecology, if you will.

Description uses sensory impressions to create accurate, even lively, word pictures of objects, scenes, people, events, ambiance, mood and emotion. While we could hardly have nature writing without description, it is most often subordinated to and supportive of narration: Insofar as narration is story-telling, it's damned difficult to spin out a compelling yarn without describing the places, people, things, moods, action and sensory impressions any story comprises. Without description, we have an empty narrative; a blank screen.

Descriptive writing is most effective when it's detailed, and when those details are rock-hard and carefully selected according to a specific purpose and point of view; descriptions whose images and impressions are clear and sharply drawn, employing the discreet use of words of color, motion, emotion, shape, sound, feel, smell, taste and (by the gods!) value. In sum, good description appeals to the senses, including, I rush to add, that most magical and meaningful sense of all, *emotion*.

For examples of masterful description, we need only thumb at random through the pages of the American nature writing classic *Desert Solitaire*, by Edward Abbey. For a straightforward (by Abbey's standards) example of physical description, take this, from the chapter "Cliffrose and Bayonet":

> The cliffrose is a sturdy shrub with gnarled trunk and twisting branches, growing sometimes to twice a man's height. When not in bloom it might not catch your eye; but after the winter snows and a trace of rain in the spring it comes on suddenly and gloriously like a swan, like a maiden, and the shaggy limbs go out of sight behind dense clusters of flowers creamy white or pale yellow, like wild roses, each with its five perfect petals and a golden center.

Analysis: The subtle creativity of this passage arises from its clarity and lyricism of description ("five perfect petals and a golden center") spiced with simile ("like a swan, like a maiden"). Even more distinct—more stylistic—is Abbey's parsimonious employment of punctuation, combined with the uncommon transposition of words ("growing sometimes" and "flowers creamy white"), netting freshness of phrase at no sacrifice to clarity. Those experienced in reading like writers will also note in this passage the judicious employment of rhythm, alliteration and repetition.

Criticism? As excerpted here, Abbey's description is purely visual; he could have further enhanced our "feel" for the cliffrose by describing its texture and aroma. However, these additional sensory descriptions may (or may not) come before or after; read the book and find out.

Farther (not further) along in *Desert Solitaire*, Cactus Ed cranks his descriptive magic to full-tilt boogie in this opening passage from "The Dead Man At Grandview Point":

> Somnolence. A heaviness in the air, a chill in the sunlight, an oppressive stillness in the atmosphere that hints of much but says nothing. The Balanced Rock and the pinnacles stand in petrified silence—waiting. The wildlife has withdrawn to the night, the flies and gnats have disappeared, a few birds sing, and the last of the flowers of summer—the globemallow—have died. What is it that's haunting me? At times I hear voices up the road, familiar voices ... I look; and no one is there.

Lovely, eh? Not merely lovely but ethereal, moody and vaguely prescient, foreshadowing the darkness of action to come. Yet, you'll be hard-pressed to identify any compositional "tricks" the author strutted out to achieve this captivating effect (except, perhaps, the disturbingly oxymoronic dissonance of "a chill in the sunlight"). Rather, the magic resides in word choice, sentence structure and cadence.

Exposition has as its goal to explain the nature of a thing—object, idea, process, animal, person, philosophy, whatever. The supporting pillars of exposition include identification, definition, description, classification, illustration, analysis and comparison and contrast—which may be employed individually or in varying combinations. Take, for example, this excerpt from the expository essay "What's In A Name?" in *Elkheart*, being but one small meander in a chapter focused on that most magical and musical of deer, the North American wapiti:

In the beginning. Which is to say, quite a long while ago, way back when the Cervidae, or deer family, were hot into the process of evolving themselves into the various species of artfully antlered, high-wired wildings we know and love today—somewhere along in there, farther back in time than the myopic human mind can comprehend—elk appeared as a distinct genus (*Cervus*): smaller than moose, but larger than deer and caribou. Like so many other bio-beginnings, that little drama most likely premiered in central Asia, perhaps at the broad green feet of the haughty Himalayas. In time, numbers of these prototypical elk spread westward, across endless Asia and into Europe, adapting to local conditions—climate, habitat, predators—as they went, evolving minor differences in morphology (physical appearance) and behavior. These became the red deer—the archetypal species of modern elk (*Cervus elaphus elaphus*). Meanwhile ...

In this excerpt (without considering the effectiveness of their employment) we get description, scientific classification, comparison-and-contrast, geographical and temporal origins, tidbits of evolutionary history—and plenty of good old et cetera. Beyond that—beyond basic employment—what you do or don't do in an effort to make straightforward exposition more palatable, colorful and memorable is a matter of personal preference: a matter of style. (Note also the use of such utterly standard stylistic conventions as providing parenthetical explanations of unfamiliar words and terms immediately following their first appearance, and highlighting scientific names with italics; there are some rules we just *can't* break.)

Argumentation, also called polemics, incorporates evidence, example, logic and emotion to convince readers of the veracity of your point of view—and simultaneously, necessarily, to rebut if not refute opposing views. A common (but by no means requisite) approach is to (1) introduce the primary point to be argued, often via a straightforward thesis statement, (2) break the primary point into component parts, (3) make your arguments, (4) present obvious opposing arguments likely to occur to readers, (5) rebut those arguments as best you can and (6) wrap things up and get the hell out while you're ahead.

Turning again to *Desert Solitaire* for example, I refer you to "A Polemic: Industrial Tourism and the National Parks," wherein Abbey argues *against* the growing commercial trend to "industrial tourism" in our parks, while arguing *for* the exclusion of private vehicles from America's national parks as a substantial cure. After opening with a cheery description of the delights of working as a seasonal park ranger, and professing his desire to make a "career" of it, Abbey introduces his core argument—the heart of the chapter—with a succinct theses statement:

> [However] there is a cloud on my horizon. A small dark cloud no bigger than my hand. Its name is Progress.

And the primary vehicle of negative "Progress" in the parks, Abbey proposes straightaway, is the automobile. Warming quickly to his task, the author invests the next several pages in delineating his arguments—calling on anecdote, history, statistics, predictions, even jokes to make his points, concluding with specific examples of the irreparable harm roads and automobiles have already done to the pristine nature of eight western national parks and monuments. That done, and using such soft-shoe lead-ins as "It will be objected" and "I can foresee complaints," the clever old curmudgeon presents several logical-seeming and predictable arguments *against* banning cars from parks—then, by showing the flaws in those arguments and offering workable alternatives, reduces them

all to intellectual campfire kindling. For an archetypal model of
the effective and entertaining use of argumentation in the essay
form, I can think of no finer example than "A Polemic: Industrial Tourism and the National Parks," particularly since so
many of Abbey's predictions, made decades ago, tragically
have come true.

Narration, or story-telling, is the bulwark of literary nature
writing, recounting as it must in riveting (highly selective)
detail an event or related series of events. As Robert Frost
emphatically suggests: "Any work of art must first of all tell a
story." And even as narration is a necessary ingredient in any
effective essay-story, so are the other three categories of nonfiction, especially description, major ingredients of narration.
Of which (narration) there are but two species:

First is *simple narration*—the straightforward, chronological
unfolding of a story line. It's the easiest to write, the easiest for
readers to follow and, until you have the steady feet of experience firmly beneath you, the easiest to sell and publish. (In
journal writing or other "for your eyes only" practice, con-
trarily, experimentation and s-t-r-e-t-c-h-i-n-g is the name of
the game.)

The second narrative approach, *narration with a plot*, is
rarely chronological, more often constructed according to
some deviously artistic plan, employing such common fictional techniques as flashback, foreshadowing and suspense.

Any essay, advises Arizona ethnobotanist and nature writer
Gary Nabhan (*The Desert Smells Like Rain*), "is obviously linear
in the sense that you read fifteen pages from one through
fifteen, but you can plant an image in part two that flowers in
part four, and introduce its pollinator in part one." This
"planting" is fun for all concerned, rendering narration-with-
plot the chosen form for the creative personal narrative: a

primary story line frequently and smoothly interrupted by side-trips into description, exposition, argumentation, even (why not?) campfire philosophy, the whole works judiciously spiced with figurative language, quotes, anecdote and such-like. The foregoing "Knee-Deep in Its Absence" is a modest example of both narration with plot and the loose parameters and glorious freedom of the personal essay. As that bit demonstrates, "plot" in nature writing doesn't necessarily (though it can) carry suspense or mystery, but more often merely suggests something a tad more elaborate than a straightforward tell. In that example, the structure is story within story within story.

By way of review, the four basic categories of nonfiction writing are:

Description—drawing precise, detailed, evocative, sensate word-pictures.

Exposition—explaining or informing.

Argumentation—not necessarily (though it can be) a heated attack, but merely an attempt to persuade.

Narration—story-telling, which can be presented either in a simple, chronological style, or as a more creative and complex narration with plot.

Commit the acronym DEAN to memory: All four are common elements—mix and/or match—of not just the narrative nature essay, but all serious nonfiction writing. When you read as a writer, keep an eye bulged out for DEAN and how its various components are employed, separately and in mutual support, and how they function to good, or not-so-good, effect.

Regarding the transfer of all this to writing—I (for one) don't think about DEAN at all during first-draft scribbling, but only during subsequent revision.

Optional exercises

Exercise 1: Select a published nature essay of any length, by anyone other than yourself, and read it through once—quickly, nonanalytically—to get a preliminary feel for the piece and a sense of its premise. Note your initial reactions. Now read it again, slowly, carefully and thoughtfully, attempting to identify its various elements—particularly the four foregoing categories of nonfiction, DEAN, and the component parts of each. And while you're about it, examine the various DEAN elements as "meanders," thinking about how each adds to, or detracts from, the progress and impact of the whole; how they facilitated your initial quick-read reactions. How would you—or could you—make improvements?

Hint: Photocopy the essay to be analyzed, or buy a cheap used paperback, so you can highlight passages and make notes—about what works, what doesn't and why—as you read. I do this with all my "serious" reading, having long ago learned that the simple act of highlighting facilitates both comprehension and memory.

Exercise 2: Repeat Exercise 1 precisely, but this time use an essay of your own; preferably one you've not read in ages. Strive for objectivity. Should your critical analysis reveal omissions or flaws, revise accordingly.

The point: The more facile you become at recognizing—and the more familiar you become with the dynamic workings of—the basic elements commonly employed in essay writing, and the more clearly you come to see how those elements fit together to form a coherent whole and to further a convincing conclusion, the more knowledgeable, comfortable and confident you'll be in structuring, critiquing, revising and improving your own writing.

Exercise 3: To sharpen both field observation skills and narrative writing, professor Florence R. Shepard always had her students write a "moving description" of some element of nature without saying how it made them feel. "You don't have to tell readers how a sunset makes you feel. *Show* them how it makes you feel via description." Try it if you dare.

Writing as Art

"Out There," with
Thomas Aquinas Daly

"DAVE ... COME check this out."

My friend Tom Daly and I have just spent a grand September morning exploring the big old mountain that rears up behind my Colorado cabin, and are headed back down when my bearded buddy, who's drifted off a ways, calls for me to come and see whatever it is he's found. After a week of practice, I rather know what to expect.

"Check this out," Tom repeats, his voice quiet but with an audible edge of excitement as he runs a hand up and down the chalky white trunk of a quaking aspen, tracing the vertical shadow-line of the sun. "*That* side of the tree is in light. *This* side is in shadow. *That* side is one color. *This* side is another. The difference is subtle, yet it's *everything.*"

No, my friend isn't drunk, drugged or crazy—he's an artist.

Matter of fact, this rough-talking, hard-walking outdoorsman and farmer from upstate New York is one of America's most profoundly talented landscape and still-life painters. He also makes artful longbows, fashions fly rods from bamboo, carves duck decoys and builds fishing boats. Having made his latest point—just one among a running litany of didactically artful details, all of which I'm instructed to pass along later to my artist spouse—we move on.

Thomas Aquinas Daly was born in 1937 in Albany, New York. He grew up in Niagara Falls, graduated from the University of Buffalo, worked twenty-three years as a commercial lithographer and art director, fathered six children, lives with his wife, Christine, and their twin teen-aged boys on an upstate working farm and has been painting professionally since 1978.

Watercolors are Tom Daly's passion and triumph—he takes the medium, so often and so erroneously associated with amateurs, to previously unconquered heights of creative professionalism—though he also produces stunning oils, etchings and aquatints and is one of only a precious few contemporary "sporting" artists whose work is celebrated by the "fine arts" community as well. In recent years Tom's paintings have been featured in the pages and on the covers of *Gray's Sporting Journal*, *Bugle* and other discerning outdoor magazines, and enthusiastically celebrated by such fine-arts periodicals as *Arts*, *American Artist* and *Southwest Art*. The winter 2000 issue of *Watercolor* honored Daly with both a cover and an inside feature.

Additionally, more than two hundred of Daly's paintings—selected from a lifetime output of eight to nine hundred—are reproduced in two spectacular books, *Painting Nature's Quiet Places* (New York: Watson-Guptill, 1985; now a pricey collector's item), and *The Art of Thomas Aquinas Daly: The Painting Season* (1998), the latter including 114 masterfully reproduced paintings, and self-published by Tom and his writer/editor/artist spouse. *Season*, by my lights, is the finest art book in print, text as well as paintings.

Tom Daly's work is shown frequently in major galleries throughout the U.S., and in 1987, his solo exhibition at New York's Grand Central Art Galleries won that prestigious institution's Gold Medal, presented personally to Tom by then-President Gerald Ford.

When James Cox, Grand Central's director, says that Thomas Aquinas Daly "is being increasingly endorsed as a legitimate successor to Winslow Homer," he's accurately reflecting the growing praise for Daly within the fine arts community. But more fitting praise, knowing Tom as I do, is an analogy offered by Anthony Bannon, director of New York's Burchfield Art Center, who muses that "if churches were built for the adoration of the sportsman's landscape, the works by Thomas Aquinas Daly would be appropriate altarpieces."

In addition to Winslow Homer, other artists whose influence shines in Daly's work, and to whom he is often compared, include Charles Wilson Peale, George Inness, John La Farge, Georgia O'Keeffe, Jean-Baptiste-Simeon Chardin, Andrew Wyeth and James McNeill Whistler. Yet all this acclaim and a whole lot more has failed to fatten Daly's head, which remains hard but lean. In a long introduction to *The Painting Season*, art scholar Dr. Cassandra Langer perfectly pegs the artist and his work when she calls him "a quiet, unpretentious, taciturn and very private man" whose paintings are "as intimate and unpretentious as he is."

But to the point: In her scholarly but friendly introductory essay, "Man and Nature: A Basic Relationship," Langer draws many instructive parallels between painting and writing. As does Tom Daly in his own explanations of his works, in both of his books. It's those parallels, extracted from Daly and Langer and wired together with my own thoughts on writing as "word painting," that I'd like to "share with you" now. (A subtly condescending cliché, that one; yet entirely apropos to our present needs.)

Too bad we have only one piece of Daly's art for reference, and only a detail at that—the ineffably, immutably elegant "Beaver Ponds with Rising Moon" gracing the cover of this book (even as the original dignifies my otherwise humble home). Yet, if you mentally substitute "writing" every time Langer or Daly says "art" or "painting," you'll get the picture.

Too soon to suit me, Tom's time in Colorado ends—we've spent a week together camping, hiking, horsey-backing, bowhunting for elk (as usual, the elk won) and indulging in impromptu *in situ* nature-art lessons—and now my friend is headed home, back to family, farm and studio.

"When I'm not hunting, fishing or doing farm chores," says Tom, "I'm painting. When I return to my studio after an outdoor adventure, I'm refreshed and eager to tap the flow of ideas and emotions the experience has generated. It's never my intention to merely describe the physical attributes of a place. Instead, I strive to capture its total essence—the visceral feeling it evokes within me. My art is generally a mirror of my life experience, creating a visual diary of sorts. I'm always attuned to my surroundings and I paint images as they present themselves. A still life with apples, for instance, is the result of a chance discovery of wild apples, as opposed to a consciously predetermined selection of subject matter. Thus, my painting is so much an integral part of my existence that I find it difficult to isolate and scrutinize. It's woven into every facet of my life in some regard or another and functions as a visual manifestation of my intangible self."

Indeed, as Cassandra Langer quotes noted psychoanalyst M. H. Abrams, in reference to poetry: "A work of art is essentially the internal made external, resulting from a creative process operating under the impulse of feeling, and embodying the combined product of the poet's perceptions, thoughts and feelings. The primary source and subject matter of a poem, therefore, are the attributes and actions of the poet's own mind; or if aspects of the external world, then these only as they are converted from fact to poetry by the feelings and operations of the poet's mind."

From this, we can extrapolate that the "trick" of the effective, emotionally connective nature essay is to internalize the external—via personal participation in, and thoughtful observation of, wild nature—then re-externalize the resulting "visceral feelings" via sensory and emotionally evocative descriptive and reflective prose.

One tool Daly uses to translate his "visceral feelings" through art is the human form. By painting people—hunters, fishers, trappers, berry pickers—into his landscapes, Daly provides a vehicle for viewer induction, allowing his "readers" to vicariously inhabit his figures, thus placing themselves, as he says, "into the landscape, into the experience." To further strengthen the universalizing power of his human figures, Daly generally renders them faceless—via distance or orientation—allowing viewers subconsciously to imagine their own faces onto the painted figures and, thus, into the scene.

Conversely, in order to challenge the often narrowly preconceived expectations of sporting (hunting and fishing) art fans, as well as to "speak to" a broader, nonsporting audience, Daly frequently creates landscapes devoid of human or even animal figures, yet which, to viewers with sufficient nature knowledge and an aesthetic alertness to verisimilitude, literally lurk with animate life. In such wildly "uninhabited" Daly landscapes, one can *feel* the wildness of the pictured place; as if you were swimming in it: you can "see" the fish holding just below the water's mirrored surface, "spot" the bird hidden in the bush and sense the deer or elk back in the shadowy woods—even when none are overtly visible, and far more powerfully than if they were.

That mysterious, magical power of mental inference and transference arises from metaphor: one thing—a word, image or idea—that evokes another, entirely different thing; "different" not so much physically as *essentially*, even spiritually. When Shakespeare says "Love is a rose," he's not talking about any physical resemblance between the two, one of which after all is palpably ineffable. Rather, he's suggesting a whole universe of subtle *essential* parallels. Likewise, when Thomas Aquinas Daly paints a wild scene devoid of people or wildlife, he's relying on subtle similarities between the painted landscape and actual places his viewers have known, to suggest the hidden life within.

Such symbolic thinking, the ability to create and perceive metaphor—to think and imagine beyond the presently visible and merely literal—is the distinguishing quality of human intellect and art. For our just-becoming-human hunter/gatherer forebears, animal tracks were the premiere metaphors, evoking not only the image of a thing unseen, but a whole exciting universe of associative feelings: danger, beauty, challenge, food, clothing, security, sounds and smells. Nor has this changed. Even today, the sight of a fresh grizzly track can be even more gut-stirring than spotting the animal that made it. How and why? Because tracks, like art and artful literature, are metaphorical and mysterious, without prescribed boundaries, inviting our imaginations to run wild and free, while the actual, "literal" animal leaves nothing to be imagined, precluding the magic of mystery. Psychologically, it's a lot like lingerie.

Similarly, Daly often paints objects—clouds, trees, mountains, waterways—just as he generally paints people, supplying only, he says, "shapes that merely suggest them. This gives the image more expression than if its details were to be described verbatim. Laboring over insignificant minutiae within a landscape robs it of its potency. I prefer to see a landscape painted broadly and spontaneously, as an emotional response."

That is the art of Tom Daly's art.

That, likewise, is the artful potential of the personal nature narrative.

Like another eminent contemporary landscape painter, Montana sportsman, writer, restaurateur and publisher (Clark City Press) Russell Chatham, much of T. A. Daly's most memorable art embraces the "luminist" theme, comprising a moody, diffused, often somber background, contrasted and highlighted with a mesmerizing trace of brightness. In Daly's work, a recurring expression of the luminist icon is a full moon—or a crepuscular sun—hung low above a wild horizon, its rich buttery glow reflected, ethereally, on mirrored water. The luminist effect is hypnotic, deeply emotional and parallels, in literature, the denouement: the moment of dramatic or thematic fruition.

As it is with artful writing, so does Tom Daly reiterate that his paintings "evolve from emotion rather than logic and I can't always explain precisely where they come from. My art closely mirrors my life experience. The process of *seeing* is perpetual, and that continuous, acute observation and the emotional responses that ensue, formulate the nucleus of what I do. I spend an enormous portion of my time outdoors, compiling reference material while engaged in totally unrelated activities. Most of my ideas for paintings arrive uninvited. If I should contrive to develop a picture of a predetermined subject, in all likelihood it will disappoint. However, if I am actively involved in my environment, I will invariably have something to say about what I see in the process. Somehow, the total sensory experience becomes assimilated, and it can resurface years later, manifesting itself as an image on paper."

And of such *seeing* and *lack of contrivance* and *personal involvement* and *assimilated experience* and *delayed manifestation*, artful magic is born, as Tom says, "on paper," whether in the robe of a writer's ink or an artist's paint.

Facilitating the "realistic surrealism" that distinguishes Tom Daly's work is a technique I call "purposeful ambiguity," a kissing cousin to metaphor and equally effective in painting and writing. To illustrate: One print in my fledgling art collection, from an oil by a well-known wildlife portraitist, is a bust of a golden eagle. The anatomical detail in this work is so strikingly precise that visitors often mistake it for a photo. And that's high praise. Yet, exactly *because* of its photographic precision, highlighted by unnatural isolation—a close-up posed against a sterile "studio" background—much of its potential magic is denied.

Now, were Tom Daly to paint an eagle, he'd hang the sucker in a broody sky, in a natural setting, caught in lifelike flight—rather than frozen, out of context, in statuesque stillness. Moreover and more importantly, Daly would provide only enough detail to suggest the *idea* of an eagle, interacting with the *idea* of its environment, leaving the rest to the viewer's imagination and thus ... *Eureka!* That is the art of art.

In literature, the eagle portrait translates to the precise scientific focus of most "natural history" writing, while the Daly approach—paying special attention to such dramatic details as scene-setting, mood and metaphorical magic—equates to the literary nature essay. At the same time, and difficult as it sounds, and in fact is to manage, Daly's art maintains an impeccable allegiance to realism—in order, he says, "to ground the image's inherent spirituality in actuality."

Spirituality grounded in actuality—any nature writer who can do as much with words will never suffer for lack of praise or publication.

CHAPTER 3

Journaling Life's Journeys

How long does it take to write a good book? All of the years that you've lived. —Edward Abbey

BEFORE WE GET INTO the gritty-nitty of sculpting an essay, it seems (chrono)logical to explore the process of generating the ideas that stories, essays and books are built on. And the primary idea-tool for all creative narrative writers and all creative narrative, is the journal.

- Thoreau recorded more than a million words in journals across a quarter-century, from which came *Walden*, numerous essays and the posthumously published journals themselves.

- Peter Matthiessen, long among America's most celebrated nature writers, wrote his most successful book, *The Snow Leopard*, in traditional (time-line) journal form, molded from three months of daily entries.

- *Refuge*, the book that brought Terry Tempest Williams to literary prominence, owes both its existence and its poignant detail to decades of devoted journal-keeping, by Terry and other members of her family.

- *The Island Within*, the book that won for Richard Nelson both the John Burroughs Medal (for distinguished nature writing) and the Lannan Literary Award (for excellence in nonfiction), began as, and retains much of the immediacy and character of, a soulful field journal.

• Ed Abbey kept exuberant journals throughout his adult life, twenty-one cursive volumes comprising more than half a million words, from which 135,000 words were gleaned, hop-scotch but essentially unedited, for *Confessions of a Barbarian*, hailed by critics and readers as among Ed's finest books. Most of Abbey's score of books and several-score essays were conceived in the dirt- and sweat-stained pages of those same journals.

And so on. Examples of the importance of journal-keeping to successful writers and celebrated writing are inexhaustible.

The two basic journal-keeping approaches—to employ a bit of highly technical literary jargon—are "sketchy" and "detailed." Often as not they are combined, mix and match, according to mood and need.

The first consists of catalytic notes designed to spark more detailed memories later, allowing the writer to keep apace with fast-moving action, then reconstruct the full events in a more relaxed setting—maybe around a campfire that same night, or back home at the computer a few days later. The sooner the better.

In the detailed approach, the idea is to capture—on the spot, *in situ*, while still alive in your senses—not merely pre-cise facts, but the mood and overall "flavor" of an experience. For example, a favorite essay of my own (if nobody else's)—among the most personally meaningful and fun to write (then) and read (still today)—was drafted essentially whole-cloth in a pocket notebook across a couple of relaxed and reflective hours one August evening while camped alone in a lonely, lovely place, watching pronghorn "antelope" (techni-cally, they're not) browse and jaybirds flit beneath a churlish sky fingered with chiaroscuro ("God") light. Happily, though I wasn't "out looking for a story," I was prepared—with journal and pencil and a pint of Tullamore Dew—and leapt headlong into the mood and moment. By dusk, "Moonshine" was pretty much a done deal ... except of course for a dozen rewrites at home.

For most writers, this one in particular, such gifts of spontaneous "creativity" come only rarely. *And they cannot be forced.* But when one does *happen*, naturally and unexpectedly— when you're *out there* and that sweet little muse comes tapping at your tent flap—don't turn her away; don't miss the opportunity to write and write—in a notebook, on a roll of toilet paper, in the sand, whatever—even if you have to excuse yourself from pleasant company to do it. Back home, scratching around for memories, you'll be damn glad you did.

Again, it's not a matter of which is best—sketchy or detailed journal entries—but which is best *when*. There are times for each and both. In a fast-moving conversation, for instance, the most that most of us can manage is to record a few pithy quotes, along with sketchy physical and character portraits of the speaker(s). The same if you're climbing a mountain or kayaking a whitewater river with only occasional brief breaks in which to hurriedly scribble notes before moving on, and while you're often physically and mentally exhausted. In such dire straits it's critical to rewrite and expand your notes at the earliest possible opportunity, before the details slip forever and sadly away, like old love.

While any notes are preferable to none, when time and mood allow I say go for precise detail in description and reflection—such stream-of-consciousness recording now will make the writing process infinitely easier later, and ultimately more rewarding. Says Gary Nabhan:

> I depend upon all senses when I'm out there. Unless I do, when I get back to a cozy room with my notebook or a word processor to write something up in essay form, I won't be able

to remember the sounds ... or what the light was like. When I take a lot of notes in the field, there is a chance that some of the sounds I hear in that landscape will carry over into sounds of the words I use to describe a place. I work hard on that because I can't do that again later. Recording the weather is also important. ... The point is that there are some features of a landscape that you can't retrace later on. Bird songs, waves crashing, leaves rustling—all of these things serve as prompts for me when I'm reworking a field journal, particularly for something that I want to use later on as raw material for an essay. It's the sensory data that I want to record in detail—so that it prompts me as soon as I read it to re-experience a particular moment.

As a fire lookout with endless slow days on his hands and story ideas a'swarm in his head, Edward Abbey became a master of journal detail. Later—he told me this straight out, and I repeatedly saw the proof—all that was left to do was to copy his cursive journal entries via his old manual Corona "typing machine," expanding and editing as he worked. A final pencil edit of the manuscript, and off it went "to become some overpaid editor's problem."

For an instructive example of this incredibly direct technique, compare the following journal entry—written July 22, 1978, while living and working as a fire lookout atop Aztec Peak in Coronado National Forest, Arizona—against the published version of a section from the essay "Watching the Birds: The Windhover," as it appears in the anthology *Down the River*. First, the journal entry:

The Windhover: Watching a redtail hawk poised on the wind; wind at twenty-five to thirty-five mph; the magnificent bird balanced in space, head twitching back and forth, watching below; the bird suddenly veers down, stooping, not in a dive, but feet-first, legs dangling—disappears into pines—reappears with a small brown thing wriggling in one talon—the hawk drops or loses the mouse for a moment, which falls diagonally, blown by the wind, back toward earth—hawk plunges after, re-snatches it, swoops to the top of a pine tree—pecks at mouse—a glimpse of blood, a red flash—then gulps mouse whole, swallows, takes off again high into space, hovering about, indifferent to my movements and glasses [binoculars]. In its swift sudden descent, the bird resembles a lady in skirts jumping off a bridge.

Now, the published revision:

The redtail hawk is a handsome character. I enjoy watching the local hunter come planing through the pass between our mountain top and the adjoining peak, there to catch the wind and hover in place for a while, head twitching back and forth as it scans the forest below. When he—or she—spots something live and edible, down she goes at an angle of forty-five degrees, feet first, talons extended, wings uplifted, feathers all aflutter, looking like a Victorian lady in skirts and ruffled pantaloons jumping off a bridge.

The hawk disappears into the woods. I watch, binoculars ready. She rises seconds later from the trees with something wriggling, alive, in her right foot. A field mouse. The hawk sails high in the air. The mouse is fighting, bites the hawk on the shank (I can see these details without difficulty), and the startled redtail drops her prey. The mouse falls down and away, also at an angle of forty-five degrees, carried eastward by the wind. The hawk stoops, swoops, and recaptures the mouse a hundred feet above the tree-tops, carries it to the broken-off top of a pine, perches there, still holding the struggling mouse in her claws, and makes one quick stab of beak to the mouse's head. I see a spurt of red. The mouse is still. The hawk gulps down her lunch raw and whole, in one piece, as an owl does. *Hors rodentine.* Later, after craw and gizzard have done their work, the hawk will regurgitate a tiny ball of fur and toenails.

As Ed himself observed, "there is a kind of poetry in simple fact." And indeed there is—especially to the poet.

So, what all did E.A. do to transform journal entry to polished essay? He added and enhanced detail, mostly via colorful description. He assigned his subject a gender, personalizing the bird as "her" rather than the more distancing "it." Rearranged things a bit. And if you're wondering why the author deleted his journalistic weather observations—apparently dishonoring Hemingway's exhortation to "remember to get the weather in your goddamned book ... weather is very important"—in the next paragraph Abbey adds this bit, by way of shifting gears:

> Mighty kettledrums thunder in the distance. My wind gauge reads thirty-five knots. The trees sway, the wind booms through the forest.

Beyond "sketchy" vs. "detailed," and speaking specifically now to the nature writer, there are three distinct kinds of journals—or at least three distinct kinds of journal *entries*—which can be kept in separate volumes or in segregated sections of the same big book, as Abbey did. They are, in order of import:

- field journal
- writer's journal
- personal journal

Keeping a *field* journal benefits the nature writer in countless ways. For example:

• As a running record of long-term natural process, such as temporal and/or seasonal changes in a local ecology (the $10 word here is phenology)—say, the decades-long transition from living tree to standing snag to limby blowdown to truncated rotting corpse to rusty dust ... the varying tones of a mountainside or lakeshore or a deer's pelage through the seasons ... the first appearances of wildflowers, birds and other annual renewals, etc.

My Caroline, a talented watercolorist, keeps a skeletal phenology of our local mountain by noting significant events on a calendar. Then, each New Year's day (or thereabouts), she ritually transfers those entries to a long-term chart. Not being so diligent myself, I frequently have to ask my wife for the date the first nighthawk arrived (invariably, it's within a week of June 1, as if the birds keep calendars of their own), or the first aspen leaf went gold (as early as mid-July, though the colors don't peak until early October), or the first bull elk bugled across the river valley (the earliest is July 9, recorded in the year 2000; the norm is mid-August, coinciding with the annual onset of the rut).

• As a precise record of observed natural detail that's beyond the reach of normal memory and of no immediate use, but which could prove precious someday: the tentative body language of a curious pine marten; the incremental decay and gradual disappearance of a winter-killed mule deer; the rainbow of hues and colors reflected in and on a landscape beneath fluid cloud-shadow; the heartbreaking consumption of former wildness by housing subdivisions, shopping malls and roads.

To further enhance detailed memory, serious journal-keepers often incorporate field sketches or even watercolors, if they're capable, or (for those of us who are "graphically challenged") photos for later reference to descriptive detail. With a camera in your daypack, you too can enjoy photographic memory.

Similarly, a shirt-pocket tape recorder can be a blessing, permanently documenting such symphonic elements of the aural landscape as the crescendo of birdsong at dusk and dawn, the sibilant sighing of wind in brittle autumn aspen leaves, the happy hiss and gurgle of a downwardly mobile mountain stream, a heart-pausing explosion of thunder, a bull elk bugling (like a sustained high note on a bluesy alto sax). Back home, listening as you write, not only will your tapes supply you with precise audio detail, but hearing those sounds again will trigger a verisimilitude of mood; a simulacrum of actuality that's beautifully conducive to so-called creativity.

Even so—tape recorders, cameras, art pencils and brushes aside—as a writer, *word-painting* should be your primary goal in field journaling, not only as fodder for "real" writing later, but for the brilliant practice such unfiltered, unpressured, stream-of-consciousness scribbling affords and ...

• As a moveable feast of on-site impressions (again, interior as well as exterior) noted during your journeys in nature. These can be mere paltry sketches or as beautifully detailed as those employed in Matthiessen's *Snow Leopard*, Williams's *Refuge* and John Baker's *The Peregrine*.

• As a place to record character sketches and conversations with traveling companions (including animals and plants, if you're so inclined), plus stray thoughts and flashes of insight the fullness of which you won't likely later be capable of accurately reconstructing from memory alone.

Differing from a field journal in intent as well as content, a *writer*'s journal is a boon to any type of composition; a filing cabinet of sorts; a portable repository for haphazard bits and pieces of information and inspiration that may or may not be of immediate value but which could someday prove useful to your writing (or to your evolving *weltanschauung*), including ...

• Snippets of conversation—your own or overheard, useful for constructing or reconstructing dialect, body language and attitude as well as content. A minor example: One summer evening several years ago, while camped (due to late-arrival desperation) at the megalopolis Madison Campground in Yellowstone National Park, the bugs were something fierce. Late in the evening, at the behest of his wife who was being devoured on the hoof by mosquitoes, a shy Japanese man camped nearby shuffled over to sheepishly ask if he could use some of our "mosquito propellant." I'm yet to use that incident (other than here), but I shall someday, somehow. Meanwhile, I chuckle every time I recall it.

• Quotations gleaned from books, magazines, newspapers, movies, songs, etc. In my writer's journal, I've designated a special section for quotes, segregated into categories, including: death (a favorite topic), organized religion (a favorite target), philosophy (a favorite), love, war and more, all of it ready and waiting whenever I need to make myself sound smarter, more spontaneous and worldly than I really am.

• Citations for books and articles, plus personal contacts that may someday prove useful in research, enlivened by brief descriptions of the essence of each.

• Potential titles, opening lines, closing lines, punchlines, outlines, story ideas, book ideas, character sketches, etc.

• Miscellaneous tiddybits: jokes, song titles and lyrics (country-western is a goldmine of double-entendre and other "low" humor: "If I said you had a beautiful body, would you hold it against me?"), bits of poetry and so on endlessly.

• Homespun "book reviews" summarizing what I've learned and thought while reading for pleasure (as opposed to focused research).

A *personal* journal is not a "dear diary," but a serious log of events, conversations, thoughts, memories and by-god especially, *emotions*—a place to store autobiographical moments that may someday prove useful; a repository for "quality" thoughts and "astounding revelations," epiphanies and just plain musings.

The personal journal is a great creative confessional; a safe and secret place to think and record thoughts so intimate we don't feel comfortable sharing them even with our closest

confidants, much less printing them for all the world to see—
at the time. Thing is, times and people change, and what today
feels and sounds like painfully personal pissimony, may someday become magically profound, possibly even comic. The
point is: Don't censor yourself when writing in your personal
journal—"let it flow" (another worthless, watery, worn-out
cliché); tell the bloody, bleeding *truth*; you can always edit yourself later, should such bits ever become meat for publication.

In a variation on the personal-journal theme, some gre-
garious, uninhibited scribes find that writing long, detailed,
deeply personal letters to friends, relatives, lovers, ex-lovers,
fantasy lovers, politicians and other public and personal enemies, inspires more poignant, creative thinking than does
"writing to themselves" in a journal. They simply keep copies
of all their letters, perhaps in a ring-binder or on computer disk,
in lieu of a personal journal. (Aside: Have you ever wondered:
What the *hell* is a "lieu"? In the original Latin, it's related to
locus, or "place.") But for most of us, writing letters entails
some degree of built-in censorship and posturing; for the
really personal stuff, a journal is generally better.

A danger in personal journaling is that the self-indulgent
pedantry and the cuteness it encourages will wend its way into
finished writing you hope to have published. To quote one
nature-magazine editor: "One of the most important things
for new writers to do is to learn to distinguish between their
diaries and their essays. The submissions I see demonstrate
that many aspiring writers have not realized the difference;
probably the number one reason work must be returned."

How best to record your journals—scribbled in notebooks,
spoken into a tape recorder for later transcription, or directly on
computer disk? While some writers—primarily graduate students and other field researchers—do carry lap-top computers

with them outdoors, to me the eerie glow of a monitor and the tappety-tap-tap of a keyboard are as out of place in nature as a tutu in a cowboy bar. Even at home, for me, a personal journal tends to be a lot less personal when kept electronically. To each …

My research for *Ghost Grizzlies* involved extensive, pleasantly exhaustive field work, living out of a backpack or horse panniers while following people who'd had personal interaction with Colorado grizzlies back to the remote places their grisly dramas had played out—where we'd relax in the shade and I'd prompt them to and through a detailed and often emotional retelling. In every case I used a portable cassette recorder, scratching key notes for backup. But in the end you should use whatever techniques work best for *you*. The important thing, however you do it, is to *keep* a journal. Keep a bunch of them.

In sum, regular, purposeful journaling is among the most important disciplines a writer can and (almost) must develop. The journal provides a repository for all manner of personally generated information; it facilitates essential writing practice, including the evolution of a personal voice; and, later and forever, it's a storehouse of essay, story and book ideas.

And it's never too soon, or too late, to start. When I was young and reckless, rodeoing Marine Corps helicopters from the pitching decks of aircraft carriers in various foreign seas and ports—well, I had me some adventures. Today, I'd give anything if I'd kept detailed journals of those exciting times. But I didn't, since I had no inkling of ever becoming a writer.

All the foregoing notwithstanding, journals aren't the only source for essay and book inspiration. Once you've trained yourself to *think ideas*, you'll trip over them at life's every turn. In fact, they'll rob you of precious sleep. It's merely a matter of awareness, subliminal as well as conscious; openness to possibility. For myself and other writers I know, common extra-journalistic sources for story ideas (all of which can, if you wish, be recorded in your journals) include:

• *Newspaper and magazine bits:* Most often, it's not an entire published story I get an urge to twist around and make my own, but some little something mentioned in passing therein—a person, place, event or phenomenon. I keep a file folder of such stimulating clips, with the significant sections highlighted for quick reference. Similarly, if you watch TV or listen to radio news, make a habit of noting (in a journal or special file) anything of potential interest.

• *Travel:* Any time you take a trip into nature, keep notes (in a journal or elsewhere) as you go along, preferably without preconceptions regarding their use (which could restrictively narrow your focus). After the trip, review your notes for story ideas.

In both generating ideas and employing those ideas in essays or books, look for the uncommon amongst the common, "jewels among the dross," the unusual within the mundane; that's where freshness hides. "Everyday life" literally brims with story ideas, if only we keep our senses, and our journals, open to the possibilities.

Optional exercises

Using whatever measure of natural wildness you have ready access to, keep a detailed daily phenology for a full calendar year. At the same time, build a periodic—say, weekly, monthly or whatever you can manage—phenology of a somewhat wilder and more remote place.

The point: Either or both will provide not only the natural history information recorded therein, but lucrative practice in observation, identification, recording, interpreting, ordering, ruminating and *feeling* the natural world. And best of all, you'll be *out there.*

CHAPTER 4

Research

"A Splendid Misery"

In research, the horizon recedes as we advance ...
—Mark Pattison

JUST AS A COMPELLING NARRATIVE is the spine of all the best and most memorable nature writing, and field experience narrative's flesh, research provides the supportive ribs of nonfiction writing.

While exposition and argument are often nearly pure research, even narration and description can (often must) be anchored by carefully researched facts, then—and here's the tricky bit—written in such a way (the popular term is "creatively") as simultaneously to flaunt and hide all that research.

Example: In *The Nearby Faraway*, I open with a story of walking in the forest and suddenly finding myself surrounded by a curious trio of tiny black bear cubs, their mother nearby but blessedly unaware of my presence. After establishing my predicament via a straightforward tell (in present tense to enhance immediacy, reader involvement and tension), I transition into a meandering explication of the natural history of black bears—including seasonal habitat needs, weight and size, regional variations, coloration, mating, gestation (delayed implantation) and denning, birth and "child-rearing," tree-climbing and cub predation, sensory abilities and more—dodging occasionally back into the action to update my situation among the bears and heighten the suspense. "How," I want my readers to wonder, "will this potentially dangerous encounter end?"

To close the piece, I build toward a denouement by brooding over all the nasty things that *could* happen should the sow discover me among her cubs—using this particular meander to insert facts about bear threats to humans, appropriate defenses and even a bit of campfire philosophy concerning why I perceive bears as special and would never want to kill one; then bring it all home with a matter-of-fact description of how the encounter concluded. And since that conclusion was—from a writer's point of view—depressingly devoid of colorful action, and given that I'd juiced the narrative up to the same electrical buzz I'd felt among the bears that day, the flat, "unfortunately happy" outcome presented a structural problem. I could, as too many "nonfiction" writers these days are quick to do in a fix, have constructed a lively lie in order to cap the bit with a bang. Instead, I opted to brighten an otherwise dull climax with bare truth and ironic humor, confessing that in the retelling if not in the happening, I longed for a livelier outcome. A writer rarely knows—"swimming under water and holding your breath," as F. Scott Fitzgerald phrased it—but it felt right, it sold (several times in fact) and I've heard no complaints.

The point: While I did all I could to make it sound and seem—not via misleading implication, but through a smooth and natural presentation—as though I knew "by heart" all that bear biology I wove into the story, the fact is that most of it came from research and interviews with experts. Even the things I did know, I double-checked. After this fashion, and no matter the genre, much of the *art* of writing is disguising the *craft* of writing.

How much research is enough? A lot more than you might like to think, or to undertake. Adventure-travel writer Tim Cahill jokes (not joking at all) that many of his magazine pieces incorporate enough research for a book. And Bud Guthrie, in researching *The Big Sky*, took so many notes that he "had to take notes on the notes" in order to make sense of it all. In my turn, I read predaciously, rarely just for pleasure but most always for research (which, happily, is generally a pleasure) and always with a HiLiter in one fist. At some point, depending on the scope of the project, I review my highlighted books, articles and journals and transfer the usable bits to the computer.

But I'm getting a little ahead of ourselves. Here, for your consideration, is a basic research plan, suitable to any scope or species of writing project. Certainly, it's not the *only* way to come at it, but one way that works.

Inventory on-site resources: What do you have already on hand that may prove useful to this project? Journals and field notes, memories and anecdotes, photographs and audio or video recordings should and in fact must see you through the essential narrative portion of the project. After that—to fuel all those edifying and electrifying "meanders," consult your clip file, your own previous writing on similar topics, your home library, the Internet and so on. That done, determine what you need to go out and hunt down—and do it.

External research: My initial "outside" research chore for any writing project (this one included) is to inventory the competition—find out what others have written on the same or similar topics—*not* in order to steal ideas or write a rip-off, but rather to plot those previous footprints so that I can step between and beyond them; to do it differently, that's my goal. Should I happen upon some useful information along that trail—most often in the form of references to primary sources worth investigating—that's a bonus.

At your local public and/or college library, start with the periodicals index, searching for magazine or journal articles addressing your topic. Next, with wish-list in hand, visit the magazine morgue and disinter all salient-seeming articles, study the lot and photocopy all promising sources for further study at home. Here again, always check the author's bibliography as a guide to additional research leads.

Done with periodicals, move on to the book index, searching for credible references appropriate to your topic. Peruse these as well, adding the best of the lot to your take-home booty. (Hint: To save time when searching for a few small specifics in large texts, check the table of contents and index for promising leads to what you want, and go directly there. There's no law, written or moral, saying a writer must read every word of every book she quotes from or lists in her bibliography.)

Homework: Thus armed, for a week or so of evenings (mornings, when I'm fresh, are for first-draft writing; afternoons are for revision; evenings for reading and research), study your resources—everything you've found in print— highlighting, taking notes and "cogitating" the works.

Find an expert: With the sizable chore of "print research" completed (for now), it's time to sniff out an expert consultant (the bigger the better) who's qualified and willing to give you a few minutes of telephone time. To speed things along, to appear more professional and to make the most of a short interview, I hit my experts with a prepared list of questions. At some point I usually bring up widely accepted pertinent "facts," plus the opinions and hypotheses of other authorities I've read or spoken with, asking in each instance for confirmation or refutation. Why bother? Because, above all else, editors hate to receive letters from readers saying "You blew it, dummy!" And I assure you, the world is populated with people gleefully poised to write just such letters. As a professional, you can own nothing more valuable than a solid reputation for truth and accuracy.

A caution regarding interview etiquette: Professional politeness demands that you defer to your informants. Don't just call someone cold and start asking questions (and *never* mail anyone a manuscript requesting a critique unless you've set it up ahead of time). By all means, have your questions ready, just in case you catch your prey in a talkie mood, but ask first if there's a more convenient time for you to call back, offering your best guess as to how much time you'll need.

To make sure I get things right, I generally ask permission to use a phone recorder, offering assurances that if I'm told something is "off the record," it will be. (In some states, secretly recording a telephone conversation is a crime.)

Finally, if the informant offers anything substantial and I determine to quote her in print, I ask if she'd like to see a draft of at least the portion of the story including her comments, in context, for verification. In addition to basic professional courtesy, this accomplishes two important goals: It puts the expert at ease, facilitating a more honest and open interview; and it gives your source a chance to correct any errors you may have made in interpretation or transcription, as well as to recast and improve on what she said "off the cuff."

In general: When researching, dig simultaneously deep and wide. Breadth involves consulting as many different— and different types of—sources as possible: print, Internet, personal interviews plus any other opportunities that present themselves. Depth means not just sifting the surface, but digging halfway to China. Gather enough research so that, come culling time, you can afford to be selective. And the primary values you should be selecting for are originality and reliability.

The two basic types, or ranks, of research are *primary* and *secondary*. Primary research comes straight from the godhead, as it were, including ranking experts and/or professional papers written by same. When you're selecting authorities to consult, don't short-change yourself; why settle for the local game warden as your expert on bears, when you can just as easily phone, or e-mail, a nationally known bear biologist? You'd be surprised how accessible most experts are—most of whom are researchers, not writers, and will welcome your help in getting their work, and their names, in print—if only you ask politely.

Secondary research is derivative. Incredibly, I occasionally see writers quoting me, from some book or article, as an authority on one thing or another. Certainly, because I try hard to get my facts from primary sources and get them straight, they're generally reliable. Yet, by quoting me, these writers are announcing publicly that they're settling for second-hand information that's perhaps flawed by personal biases or faulty interpretation, when they could almost as easily check my text citations or bibliography and consult the same primary sources I used.

Be neither lazy nor hazy in your research, but thoroughgoing and adventurous. Yet know when to stop researching and start writing—and make yourself do it. Otherwise, you'll end up chasing a "forever-receding horizon" of superfluous knowledge.

Regarding research technique: You can save a lot of time and energy by outlining or otherwise getting a good tight fix on your primary, secondary and tertiary points before start-ing, thereby avoiding pointless wanderings through useless literature.

Similarly, biting off too broad a topic not only necessitates extraneous research, it ruins a lot of books and essays, sacri-ficing depth and style to the superficiality required to cram too much info into too small a space. A spin-off here is the tendency for beginners—and some slow-to-learn veterans—to submit over-length articles and books, hoping editors will buy them anyhow and take on themselves the hard work of carving out all that excess fat. (Adding insult to injury, the same windy writers often whine like chainsaws when that necessary cutting *does* get done, making themselves unpopular with that editor forevermore.) But in most cases, editors won't do your cutting for you and entertain little respect for writers who can't or won't take direction.

In the end, if research promises or proves to be a drudge, you're either not cut out for nonfiction writing or you're writing on the wrong topic. Write about what you crave to learn about, and your research will be a joy.

In *The Passionate Fact*, author and performance story-teller Susan Strauss quotes National Public Radio's *A Prairie Home Companion* host, master yarn-spinner and croaky crooner Garrison Keillor as remarking in an interview: "If you don't have that passion to tell a story, you will settle for telling it not very well. But, if you have the passion … it becomes a wonderful problem in your life—a wonderful problem [note Keillor's clever employment here of repetition for emphasis] like being in love. It becomes an irritation, a splendid misery."

A splendid misery … *that's* what research should be. Gary Snyder—poetic raconteur and roadkill connoisseur—would dub research "good work," his highest honor.

CHAPTER 5

Doing It

The Willful Act of Writing

The writing process is akin to any process of creation—there is pleasure in the conception and much discomfort in the growth.
—John A. Murray

WE COME NOW to the mechanical reality of writing—the essential act of conceiving ideas, converting those ideas to words and committing those words to paper (or, more often these virtual days, to magnetic tracks on a computer disk).

As noted earlier, many of the best nature writers work directly from carefully kept journals: indexing, culling, cutting and pasting, then filling in the gaps with research, ordering, interjecting, verifying, constructing transitions and otherwise smoothing and polishing. It's a technique used to excellent ends by Thoreau, Abbey, Nelson, Williams, Zwinger, Nabhan and so many more.

Of course, working from journal notes isn't the only way to write. Some writers always, and all writers sometimes, dive in cold. Hemingway, whose fiction and nonfiction alike relied heavily on personal experience, prepared detailed outlines and writing schedules—"project plans," he called them—and proceeded accordingly, revising heavily as he wrote, getting every sentence, every paragraph perfectly polished before moving along to the next, confessing in *A Moveable Feast* that "It often took me a full morning of work to write a paragraph."

Similarly, A. B. Guthrie, Jr. was downright proud that he'd once spent half a day composing just one "troublesome key sentence" of dialogue for *These Thousand Hills*. (A bunch of unemployed Montana cowboys had been reduced to holing-up for the winter in a tiny, windowless frontier cabin, from which they occasionally ventured out to poison wolves for survival income—work they all hated. When one wondered aloud how their young boss, the novel's protagonist, had talked them into this painful scheme, the answer—Guthrie's "troublesome key sentence"— came back: "A man with a purpose don't lack for a party.")

Likewise, Flaubert bemoaned the fact that he'd needed six full weeks of hard labor to compose and revise just the first thirteen cursive pages of *Madam Bovary*.

Me: I prefer to write first drafts straight through, without interruption, fast as I can go, not stopping even to correct typos or dig up missing facts—like a sculptor heaping up a preliminary mound of clay; "vomit it all out" is a term I've heard myself use—until I have a complete draft, usually way too long, at which point the sculpting begins.

We've seen Abbey's preferred essay technique: running detailed journal entries through a typewriter, revising and expanding as he went, then line-editing the typed script and sending it off. Even for those few among us who could manage to write to their own and their editor's satisfaction with such minimal revision, such a "relaxed and natural" approach would lead to prompt professional death, in that no sane editor these overworked days would look past the first page of such a messy, scribbled-over manuscript ... unless of course you're Edward Abbey, which no one again will ever be.

In sharp contrast, John A. Murray—a prolific nature writer, an even more prolific editor of literary nature-writing anthologies and author of *The Sierra Club Nature Writing Handbook*—uses the Hemingway technique: working out a detailed plan in advance, including a full, formal outline and production schedule—*X* many pages to be written and polished per day—then sticks tight to it, writing hard and fast. Moreover, says John: "When I begin writing, I always write the opening and the closing first. Many other writers do this. These openings and closings remain pretty much the same through any subsequent editing changes. They form, to use a metaphor, the airport from which I depart and the airport at which I will land. The outline then becomes a sort of flight plan from which I ordinarily deviate very little."

Certainly, this works for John—he's the fastest writer I know—just as it works for those "many others" he mentions, and so it could possibly work for you, assuming you *know* the best opening and closing a priori and enjoy whipping yourself to work each day, no matter what. For me, alas, such a militaristic attack on writing simply doesn't work. I don't always know the opening and rarely know the closing before the writing starts. Nor can I think of any better way to infect myself with a terminal case of writer's lockjaw than to force myself to fabricate an opening and closing first and try to wedge a story between—or to demand of myself a certain number of pages per day no matter the mood or distractions.

To the contrary, I prefer a looser, more casual arrangement that facilitates my essays and books (essentially) writing themselves. I rarely know the opening until I'm well along, nor the closing until I'm there. But we'll reserve further such "in and out" details of process for a chapter all their own. Here and now, let's just say that for me (at least), among the greatest joys of writing for a living is that I *don't* have to meet any self-imposed work schedules (only editor- and poverty-imposed deadlines); creating a daily production plan for myself would be to appoint an internal taskmaster, spoiling all the fun and crippling my motivation. Might as well be back in the Marines.

Expanding from specific to general, here's a time-proven, open-ended, ten-step writing process you might find felicitous—by no means chiseled in marble yet a reliable routine that can help you get into, through and happily out of most writing projects, from tersest essay to tumescent tome.

1. Conception: Generate a story idea.

2. Outline: The archetypal academic outline is a detailed and formal affair plotted on paper. When writing a book— if for no other reason than to facilitate writing a book *proposal*—I loosely follow this formalized form. But when writing articles and essays, my outlines are a lot less structured and detailed; generally just vague, loose and limber plans of approach, written only in my head and open always to spontaneous evolution.

But no matter how you outline, you first must identify, narrow, expand, massage, refine and clarify a primary theme (premise). Second, think through and list the main points you wish to make, arranging them in logical order of presentation. Third, list subtopics under each main topic. Research and writing now become simply a matter of filling in the outline, in any old order you wish.

Hint: If you're having trouble getting started, write the easiest bits first; often, all it takes to break through writer's block is to start writing ... *anything*.

3. Research

4. Boil it down to notes

5. Organize your notes and revise your outline if and as necessary

6. Write a first draft

7. Revise

8. Revise

9. Revise

10. Revise some more

Now we're cooking.

Optional exercises

To determine whether you're a type A (Hemingway/Murray) or type B (Petersen) writer, try assembling an essay by first composing a lead and close, then sandwiching the story between, polishing as you go. Now (soon as you're rested) write a second essay, starting wherever it feels good and spider-webbing out from there, working without polish until you have a complete first draft.

Second and similarly, in writing projects of comparable length and difficulty, compare working with a formal written outline against an informal mental outline.

Point: In writing, the concept of "best" is rarely as valid, meaningful or workable as "personally preferable." To adapt and maintain just one way of going about it without ever trying others is like one-legged dancing.

CHAPTER 6

What's in a Title?

Titles are shadows ...
—Daniel Defoe

INDEED THEY ARE—specifically, in the instances of essay and book titles, *fore*shadows, hinting provocatively at what's to come.

As an analogy to ease us into a discussion of crafting good titles, consider the carnival barker—that colorful character who stands out front of the bigtop, shouting and flailing his arms, doing his darndest to grab the attention of passers-by and coax them in for the show. What makes or breaks a barker is his (or, I suppose, though I've never seen one, her) ability to accomplish this miracle of persuasion in the few moments a potential customer is within visual and verbal reach.

Like a barker, the title of your essay or book must attract attention and coax a disinterested audience in off the noisy media midway to view your show. And you don't have long to do it. When a title's persuasive value is weak, browsing readers (including acquiring editors) may pass you by in favor of a writer whose pitch is more compelling. Conversely, an *effective* title—one that sounds a note of universal recognition and interest, that poses an intriguing question, that elicits a chuckle or just plain *sounds good*—that title will grab the attention of potential readers and have them under your canvas straightaway.

An effective title accomplishes three things. It:

- Catches the browsing reader's attention
- Foreshadows what's to come
- Prompts readers to keep reading

No set rules dictate how you accomplish these three goals. Like wine, an effective title has no rigid shape of its own, but adapts itself to the form of its container. Depending on the mood of the work it names and the personality of the target market, a title can be:

Straightforward and descriptive: *A Field Guide to Writing Fiction* (Guthrie).

Indirect, even veiled, suggesting the theme but leaving the reader to wonder about the precise nature of the theme and how it will be handled: *Beyond the Aspen Grove* (Zwinger).

Esoteric—beyond the merely indirect; designed to prick the reader's curiosity while relying on an explanatory subtitle or "read-line" (an extended subtitle) to bring the picture into focus—*Heartsblood: Hunting, Spirituality, and Wildness in America.*

Playful—enlisting word games: "Of Rogues and Wretches, Ruffians and Riffraff" (alliteration).

Familiar/allusive—based on a well-known cultural theme, often arising from the realms of literature or art, and often twisted for originality or humor: "Through a Cave Darkly" (Tim Cahill); *The Nearby Faraway* (backformed from the archetypal Georgia O'Keeffe painting, "The Faraway Nearby").

Or, a well-known theme can be used verbatim; for example, years ago I wrote a how-to piece (for *Mother Earth News*) on building wood fires in hearths, stoves and outdoors. My editor dubbed it "To Build a Fire"—a direct reference, via verbatim repetition—to Jack London's well-loved story by the same name. Plagiarism? Hardly. Copyright law places titles in the public domain, allowing them to be adapted and recycled endlessly. If anything, title repetition is a compliment to the original, acknowledging its ingrained cultural status.

A master of the creative title is Tim Cahill—eagerly aided, he's quick to give credit, by various magazine editors. Together, Tim and his allies have come up with such memorable titles as:

"Some Like It Cold" (dog-sledding)
"In the Valley of the Shadow of Death" (an on-the-scene report from the Jonestown murder-suicide tragedy)
"The Fit Parade" (temper tantrums among Hollywood celebrities).

Likewise, Cahill's books invariably carry intriguingly esoteric titles (which he usually explains in his prefatory remarks), including:

Buried Dreams (the biography of a mass murderer)
A Jaguar Ripped My Flesh (adventure-travel anthology)
A Wolverine is Eating My Leg (a-t anthology)
Road Fever (the chronicle of a record-setting road trip)
Pecked to Death by Ducks (a-t anthology)
Pass the Butterworms (a-t anthology)

Caution: Not all readers, sadly, are avid consumers of classic (or classical) literature. Therefore, when you play off a literary theme, even one you suppose to be commonly familiar, you risk leaving some potential readers standing outside the tent, intellectually alienated. Cahill takes this into consideration and uses not only literary themes, but music, movies, TV programs, history, famous jokes, the Bible—just about anything a vast majority of the audience he's writing for can be expected to identify with or at least to have heard of. Follow Tim's lead: Each time you sit down to compose a "familiar" title, think about the readers at whom the essay or book is aimed—their probable age, gender, education and interests, and the allusive themes most likely to tickle their collective fancy.

For example, I borrowed a Shakespeare line for the title of this chapter, confident that my slight twist on the tragically foreboding query from *Romeo & Juliet*—"What's in a name?"—would ring widely familiar. I also considered "O, that I had a title good enough," "O, how that name befits my composition!" and "What you will have it named, even that it is." But in the end, I decided all of those were too oblique even for a highly literate audience: The more familiar, the more better.

At what stage in writing an essay or book should you worry about a title? To stick with a favorite exemplar, composing good titles was literally the last thing on Ernest Hemingway's mind; he generally wrote them last. But last for Ernie meant anything but least, and the proof is in the print: "A Clean, Well-Lighted Place," *Death in the Afternoon, A Farewell to Arms, For Whom the Bell Tolls* and my favorite, *A Moveable Feast*.

Researching and composing a title after a work was completed was Ernie's way, but it isn't the only way. I jot down every title possibility that crawls under my cap as I'm researching and writing, and generally opt for one that can be repeated verbatim and with telling force somehow, somewhere—preferably in association with the denouement—in the book or essay. One prolific magazine freelancer of my acquaintance says the surest cure for an attack of mid-article writer's block is to put the troublesome piece aside for a while and brainstorm titles. For her, this midstream exercise in "writing short" helps not only to refill her creative bucket, but brings the remainder of the piece into clearer focus. Still other writers come up with a working title before they begin writing—again, to help establish and maintain focus—knowing they can always change the header later, should they stumble onto something better.

Subtitles are enlightening afterthoughts that clarify and amplify, and which are generally lengthier and more revealing than the titles they tail. A direct, self-explanatory title, such as Canadian biologist Valerius Geist's *Deer of the World,* may not need a subtitle at all. (He gave it one anyhow: *Their Evolution, Behavior, and Ecology.*) However, if you choose a title as esoteric as *The Nearby Faraway,* a clarifying and enlightening subtitle (*A Personal Journey Through the Heart of the West*) is demanded, since only fans of southwestern art can be expected to be familiar with Georgia O'Keeffe's famous painting, and even *that* is confusingly esoteric.

No matter how you go about composing them, wherever you find them, the cost in time and creative energy to come up with effective titles and subtitles is often high. Consider it a worthwhile exercise in poetry and a necessary investment in advertising.

CHAPTER 7

The Old In-And-Out

Composing Effective Openings and Closings

*How many good books suffer neglect through the
inefficiency of their beginnings!*

—Edgar Alan Poe

A RAGGEDY OLD WRITING CLICHÉ proclaims the obvious:
"Every story must have a beginning, a middle and an end." As
self-evident as it seems, this basic structural wisdom is frequently ignored—particularly regarding the ending, which
far too often is a toss-away. But we'll get to that when we get
to that. First ...

You've done your research, assembled and organized all
your pieces and bits, laid your best plans and revved-up your
hard drive—so, how to get started *writing*?

Certainly, if you *can* begin at the beginning, have at it. But
for many if not most writers, the easiest entry into a story (or
chapter)—the logical, preferable and often essential starting
point—is some anecdote or fact or bit of dialogue, some *something* you know you want to include and how you want to
say it, no matter where in the story that chip may fall. You
don't *have* to begin at the beginning.

The painter Thomas Aquinas Daly employs a similar technique, testifying: "I have found that small beginnings are sufficient to carefully and steadily start the wheels turning." And
with those wheels turning, simply work from one known

image, scene, fact, quote, anecdote, whatever, to the next. Gradually, as you assemble a good pile of passages and arrange and connect them, your essay will begin to assume the shape it naturally prefers—"writing itself." That's day one.

Day two, assuming there's more first-draft writing yet to do, in order to get restarted, my preference is to re-read, start to finish, what I wrote the day before, revising *lightly* as I go—this is not the time (for me at least) to get sidetracked into heavy self-editing. Granted, a complete re-reading takes a while, depending on the length of the piece, but it's hardly time wasted, and when you reach yesterday's end, you'll be primed for a new beginning—firmly back in the saddle, relaxed and ready to roll, seemingly without (to further mix this mess of metaphors) having ever missed a beat.

A. B. Guthrie, Jr. preferred a different restart method, cutting more directly to the chase: "If you've had a decent day," Bud advises, "it may be well to quit though you want to go on. You'll be encouraged next day to proceed with what you left undone."

Bud's sentiment is echoed by his contemporary, Hemingway, who allows as how: "The best way is always to stop when you are going good and when you know what will happen next."

As you've likely surmised, these two methods—reviewing the previous day's work, and stopping when you still know where you want to go next—are by no means mutually exclusive.

Eventually, of course, you'll have to write a lead. Whenever and however you come at it, the lead has three essential duties:

- Hook readers and keep them reading
- Set the stage (ambiance) and tone (voice) for what's to come
- State your premise (or at least imply it)

When reading as a writer, you'll note that many leads take two or even three paragraphs to accomplish the secondary and tertiary goals of setting the stage and establishing, or at least strongly suggesting, the theme. That's OK, if not ideal. But the hook must penetrate in the first paragraph, preferably in the first sentence, or you risk losing your fish.

Happily, hooking is not rocket science. A hook doesn't have to be flashy or dramatic (as witness this chapter's opening), but merely calculated (yes, calculated) to attract a potential reader's attention and hold it for a few sentences—by which time, if for no reason other than mental inertia, and unless the piece is total crap, most readers will keep on reading.

Common opening techniques include:

Colorful dialogue: "'I'll guarantee ya,' says my new friend Jason Wilson, 'the first time you see it, you'll get a rush that'll surpass anything in your entire pharmaceutical history.'" ("Yellowstone Death Watch," *The Nearby Faraway*).

Colorful quote: See the previous multi-duty example.

Colorful epigraph: An epigraph is an epigram—a short, pithy and relevant quote—used to introduce an essay, chapter and/or book, subtly setting the tone and perhaps presaging the theme. Additionally and ideally, an epigraph can serve as a smooth, connective transition from title into lead, introducing the theme in the doing. Title: "In Defense of Predators" (*Elkheart*). Epigraph: "We are kindred all of us, killer and victim, predator and prey" (Abbey). Opening:

> I'm sitting at my plywood-plank desk, out in the little office I call the Outhouse, doing what I call work, when my blushing bride comes slumping in, brown eyes tearing. I ask what's wrong.
>
> "A raven just took *all* the robin chicks from the nest down by my garden. I yelled at it and threw rocks, but it ignored me. It breaks my heart to see that kind of thing."

Of course it does, notwithstanding that the raven in question, a local bird, has nestlings of her own to feed and robin chicks are in good supply this spring.

By now, I hope readers of that piece have a taste (or distaste; in this event either is fine) for what's to come.

Thesis statement: Here's where you come right out and say (in so many words): "This is what I plan to talk about." It sounds stiff, and it can be, yet it can also be wholly effective, especially in argumentation and exposition. For example: Since the above "In Defense of Predators" was aimed primarily at predator-phobic hunters who let themselves believe that "predators are killing too many of *our* prey, so we're justified in hating and wantonly persecuting them as 'bad' animals," I could have opened with a direct thesis statement, like so:

As predators ourselves, you'd think that hunters, more than anyone else, would understand the intricate and essential predator-prey relationship and its importance to a balanced ecology. Yet, many in hunting's raggedy ranks are among the worst and most vicious of predator-phobics, looking upon carnivores as competitors, thus enemies, thus fair game for thoughtless slaughter. I am here to challenge that gutless paradigm.

That *could* have worked as a lead—most editors would have let it through—though I don't believe it would have hooked nearly so many readers, even among crusty hunters and especially not among women, compared to the gentler, anecdotal raven/robin lead with its broader emotional appeal. Consequently, I saved the hard-hitting thesis statement for a little farther (not "further") along, employing it to transition from the opening anecdote to the polemic that comprises the bloody heart of the thing.

Among the most brilliant examples I can muster of a thesis-statement lead is this tight brace of opening sentences from Aldo Leopold's foreword to his classic *A Sand County Almanac*:

> There are some who can live without wild things, and some who cannot. These essays are the delights and dilemmas of one who cannot.

Word picture/scene-setting: This is the "mind's eye" equivalent to a sound bite—a quick, precise and preferably pithy description of a scene or event having high probabilities of pulling readers into your story. It may clearly introduce your theme, or simply suggest it. Either way, the goal, as always, is to keep the reader reading:

> Sunset. Once more, at this magical conjunction, I found myself turning toward reflections rather than the source of light. Long shadows, stretching across my path, intensifying the gray-green of desert shrub, assured me that I would arrive about on time. (Florence Krall Shepard, *Ecotone*)

Anecdote: In this application, an anecdote is a brief true story intended to set the stage for the longer story to come. Anecdotes can begin without fanfare, but more often are introduced with such as "I once loved a girl who loved ..."

In medias res: Literally, "in the middle of things," where you plunge headlong into your narrative, establishing immediate bonding and curiosity in the reader's mind via the element of mystery: "At that point, I wouldn't have bet a rusty nickel on our chances of surviving the night." Who are these people, where are they and what's their predicament?

Provocative question: Here again, as so often is the case, the idea is to create a mystery that readers will want to solve. "Why do deer have antlers?"

Autobiographical memory: A personal historical anecdote. "In our family, there was no clear line between religion and fly fishing." (Norman Maclean, *A River Runs Through It*).

Joke: So long as it's funny, appropriate to your audience and somehow relates to and prefaces what comes next, almost anything goes.

There are other ways to open an essay, chapter or book, of course, but the above are among the best and (thus) most commonly used.

Another professional cliché (writers who write about writing just love the things) asserts: "After the lead, the *close* is the most important part of any story." I say: It depends.

Certainly, without a good lead you may never get your story published, and even if you should (say, you have some dirt on your brother-in-law, the editor), few will bother to read it. But once a reader is committed, I propose that the close becomes even *more* important than the lead.

How so?

The point the close makes (or summarizes and/or reiterates)—the images it evokes, the mark it leaves on the mind—determines how and if the reader will remember the story. Or its author. Have you ever read a magazine story without bothering to note the writer's name (as most readers do); then, being so impressed with how the story ended, gone back to check the byline, and maybe even remembered it? I have, many's the time. In fact, I'll hazard that the best two ways to earn name recognition with readers and editors are good endings—and good contextual jokes. Of the two, good jokes are by far the harder to come by.

No matter the tack it takes, the close should emerge naturally from the text. And most important, the close should leave readers with a feeling of closure, completion, satisfaction; a good journey well finished. By all means, avoid such insipid throw-aways as "Happy mushroom hunting!"

Proven, effective closure techniques include:

The resolution of a problem (or mystery or plot) presented earlier in the essay. This is doubly effective if the problem is introduced in the lead, so that your ending serves not only as a resolution, but closes a circle as well.

Provide a logical conclusion to a narrative storyline.

Reiterate and clarify the theme.

Conclude an argument with a bang.

Pose a thoughtful question arising from, or reflecting back upon, your theme, thus prompting the reader to think independently beyond what you've said.

An apropos quotation: The shorter the better, being punchier and thus more memorable. Dialogue—"And that's when Molly told me that I could go …"—is generally more effective than quotes lifted from print.

Title redux: Find a way to incorporate the title in your closing graph. "This, all of it, is why I speak out proudly in defense of predators." ("In Defense of Predators.")

Surprise ending: Frequently, though not necessarily, this involves a joke, overt or implied.

In medias res **(redux):** Stop abruptly and provocatively in the middle of things, leaving readers to imagine the various possible outcomes. This, I profess, is among the most potentially dramatic, thus most effective of all endings. For instance, you take a wilderness backpacking trip and *don't* return home, but end the story while you're still out there, still with unknown challenges to face and an open-ended outcome. Or, similarly, leave a critical decision open-ended (so the reader can decide).

Complete an incomplete anecdote that was begun, then interrupted, in the lead. For example, you might open with a heart-pounding tale of being trapped in an avalanche—then transition into the body of the piece, where you describe the physics of avalanches, advise how to avoid them and what to do if you're caught in one—then close by telling of your narrow escape.

Summary: A succinct and creative recounting of your main points; most effective for argumentation and exposition.

Circle back to the lead in some way other than a title redux or split anecdote. This technique restates rather than completes the lead. For example: In "Yellowstone Death Watch," I opened with that esoteric and vaguely politically incorrect quote from Jason Wilson about the "pharmaceutical-quality" natural high attendant to watching a grizzly bear chase, catch, kill and eat an elk calf. At that early stage in the story, I am the innocent novice, the listener, the student, while Jason is teller and teacher; the wise old veteran. By the time we reach the end of that longish literary journey, I've become a veteran myself, and, apropos, close by repeating Jason's opening line to a German tourist with marginal English—who, of course, can't be expected to have a clue as to what the heck I'm talking about, and in fact does not, thus creating an inside joke between readers and writer. I hope.

The *corpus* of an essay, of course, is where the real work gets done—where the plot unfolds, the action plays out, your knowledge is shared, your points well put. How, exactly, this should proceed, is the writer's challenge to unravel. To help get you started, here are three proven possibilities for structuring the body of an essay or book chapter:

Tell-tell-tell is the simplest and most straightforward way to proceed, great for how-to and workable for exposition and argumentation, but withal the least creative and most limiting (at least in the nature writing genre).

Example: If I wanted to write a story explaining how to perform an Eskimo roll in a kayak—a technique used to upright the little boat after it has accidentally flipped in dire straits—I might open with an anecdote about capsizing in a nasty bit of whitewater, caught unawares while my attention was distracted by a red-tailed hawk's nest in a cottonwood tree on the shore, then saving myself from possibly drowning, or at least having to abandon my boat and swim for it, by executing an instant expert Eskimo roll. With readers thus intrigued, I'd then plunge headlong into the didactic body of the piece, and tell-tell-tell, to wit:

Tell 'em what you're going to tell 'em (lead): "The roll that saved the day that day—and that might just save your day someday—entails five quick-fire steps: stabilize, position paddle, overhead stroke, hip-snap, follow-through."

Tell 'em what you want to tell 'em (body): Here, each of the five steps is explained in careful detail.

Tell 'em what you told 'em (close): A straight summary, renaming (simply listing) the five steps in order, and maybe returning somehow to the opening anecdote by way of graceful escape.

Used in expository or polemical nature writing, tell-tell-tell works much the same as it does in the how-to example above, except that you're generally explaining how some natural phenomenon works—an avalanche, the elk rut, a salmon spawn, a volcanic eruption, the ecologically devastating "island effect"—rather than how to do something. And rather than clearly defined steps, your tellings should unfold in a flowing, lyrical progression.

Pull a train: This too is a fairly straightforward approach, but with wider application to nature writing, useful in narration as well as exposition and argument; a classic story outline form. Imagine a train, complete with locomotive, passenger cars (with people peeking out the windows) and a caboose.

The locomotive is your lead, the cars are your primary points, the passengers within the cars are sub-points, the tie-links between cars are transitions and the caboose is all she wrote. An advantage here is that you can pretty much mix and match any lead technique you like with any close. For instance, the engine might be *in medias res*, and the caboose a word picture. The train cars could be the stages in an explication, the primary points of an argument or a logical progression of events in a narrative storyline. The passengers, of course, are subpoints, anecdotes and other meanders.

Full-circle is my own old favorite. It's infinitely flexible, perfect for the rambling essay form and felicitous to creativity. At the top of the circle (12 on a clock face), you open with something overtly memorable—a catchy phrase or familiar song title, a particularly profound epigram, an interesting but incomplete (split) anecdote, a few lines of intriguing dialogue or poetry, a sterling word-picture—virtually anything, so long as it will pop immediately to reader memory with the assist of a calculated catalyst at the story's end.

With the lead established, now transition into, and work through, the body of your essay—then, as the end comes in sight, return suddenly to the opening theme or image with a degree of surprise, coming at it from some unexpected angle, for a wham-bang close. For example, the (thrice) previously trotted-out "better than pharmaceuticals" quote that opens and closes "Yellowstone Death Watch" soundly completes a circle. Your circuitous goal is to lead the reader so far away from the opening that the unsuspecting soul has (temporarily) forgotten all about it; thus, it comes as a pleasant surprise— like an old friend unexpectedly encountered in a strange city—when it reappears suddenly, without warning, in the final paragraph or (better yet) final sentence. Of course, the circle-back close must do the essential work of any ending, and leave readers with a satisfying feeling of completion.

Optional exercises

By way of review: An opening must entice, an ending must complete and the body must fulfill. Study the heads, torsos and tails of several nature essays—your own and others—to see if you can identify the in-and-out techniques employed and determine, to your tastes, whether they work, and if the head and tail are satisfactorily connected. If you spot a weakness, how would you correct or improve on it? Would another in/out technique—perhaps one of those outlined above—have worked better?

Similarly, using an old essay of your own, lop off the original head and tail and experiment with various alternatives.

CHAPTER 8

Getting Personal

Befriending the Vertical Pronoun

*A story should be a personal thing, not just an account of one day
after the next. Those are just the facts. Life is what happens
between the facts.* —Robert Perkins

IN HIS STURDY TEXT *On Writing Well,* so timelessly popular
among writing teachers, William Zinsser advises nonfiction
writers to "let the nature of the material determine whether or
not to put yourself into the story, and, if so, to what extent."

Personal nature narrative, by definition, *demands* that we
put ourselves into our stories, *way* in. The best nature writing
reveals and deals with the juncture between the exclusively
human world (culture), and the suprahuman natural world
that shaped and continues to nourish us, spiritually as well as
physically, if only we are open to it. Moreover, as Florence
Shepard lays it out: "Writing about our own self-knowledge
and experience taps the genius in each of us and impels us to
act creatively. I further propose that autobiography leads us
inward, toward self-understanding, and outward toward a
more complete understanding of the human condition. We
write for others who read and listen to us, but we also write
for ourselves, and listen to ourselves."

Or, as Annie Dillard would have it: "Language is like a beam
of light on Venus. There, on Venus, heavy atmospheric gravity
bends light round the entire circumference of the planet,

enabling a man, in theory, to see the back of his own head."
(And a woman hers, fair to assume.)

The trick to writing first-person, autobiographically or
narratively, is doing it well—with "well" in this instance
describing a carefully balanced ego act. Turn-of-the-century
naturalist Ernest Thompson Seton perfectly captures the two-
armed aspect of personal nature narrative when he notes in
the preface to his four-volume masterpiece, *Lives of Game
Animals*: "A natural history must be a vast collection of reliable
facts—plus a personality. The facts herein are the best available. Whether the personal touch they bear is acceptable,
remains to be seen."

I propose that the best nature writing—the real, gritty, time-
less, literary goodstuff—owes its success to achieving Seton's
"acceptable personal touch." Likewise, much of what fails,
fails for want of that touch. To master personal writing is to
master ego acrobatics; treading the edge of the abyss between
projecting a strong, charismatic personality and an annoying
solipsism. Contrary to what many aspiring (and some established) writers seem to believe, everything that pops into our
heads is *not* worth committing to print.

One unfortunately negative example that comes readily to
mind—and whose author and title shall remain benevolently
anonymous here—was a slender book intended to instruct
outdoor novices in the subtleties of, let us say, "personal
hygiene," when wayfaring in the woods. Thanks to a cleverly
scatological title, the book became a minor bestseller in outdoor circles—yet, all the truly useful info it contains could
have been squeezed onto a single page, and the writer's style
is cloyingly supercilious.

Another, more precise, example of the sort of auto-infatua-
tion we must strive to avoid in personal writing (and in life)
is brilliantly illustrated in an introduction to a nature writing
anthology published several years ago (and now safely out of

print). In the following sample—not jerked radically out of context but fairly representative, I believe, of the whole—witness not only the prolificity of what Hemingway calls "the vertical pronoun" (I, me, my), but also the self-absorbed, substantially insubstantial way those self-directives are employed:

> While I admit that the contents of [this book] could be a little skewed, I insist that the distortion was done with the best of intentions. Because I'm a college professor, I chose contemplation over adventure. Because I'm a westerner, I preferred landscapes that lie beyond the hundredth meridian. Because I live in a desert environment near the Sierras, I naturally read more desert and Sierra essays than pieces about the Everglades and Adirondacks. Because I care about conservation and preservation, I especially honored any writer who respects the land. Any time, any place will do—but I acknowledge the fact that certain times and places interest me more than others.

The almost unavoidable reaction is: What about your *readers'* interests, dear professor? What happened to *them*? To *us*?

Faced with such as the above, Abbey would (and did) counsel us to speak "not *to* our audience (who wants to listen to lectures?), but *for* them, expressing their thoughts and emotions through the imaginative power of our art." Award-winning natural history writer David Quammen expresses the same sentiment when he observes that "Too much of the writing I see is solipsistic and not connected to readers. ... I don't believe writing exists for its own sake or for writers to hear the sound of their own voices, but to connect with readers and to persuade."

The professor, alas, neither connects nor persuades. Moreover, clearly intoxicated on the sound of her own voice, she "smears herself all over the damned page," as Bud Guthrie would (and did) put it. And frankly, it's not easy *not* to. Yet, a requisite for successful first-person writing commands the writer to be invisible, to crawl inside the reader's head and become the universal Every(wo)man; not, rather, to blather on about her- or himself in ways sure to interest no one else. (And here we are, mucked—intentionally, demonstratively—in convoluted "gender-correct" verbiage. While we could avoid such bogs by using plural rather than singular pronouns, that's yet another dead-end "correctness" trap.)

To make readers feel they're reading about *them*selves, even as you're writing about *your*self—is perhaps the greatest creative challenge you'll face in personal narrative.

That said, and flipping now to the bright side of the first-person penny, consider this next bit, from *Confessions of a Barbarian: Pages from the Journals of Edward Abbey*, written when Ed was twenty-five, at the time unpublished and recently unmarried:

> Even now, almost two months after her departure, I can still experience, when properly stimulated by some appropriately associative sensation—a song, a walk under the trees, a certain obscure fragrance, like fermented rose juice—the need for Jean. I remember her suddenly, deeply, poignantly, and long for a look at her (tho I can hardly remember her face) and for the feel of her warm heavy solid body in my arms, pressed against me, and the smell and tickling caress of her hair against my face.

Although that graph, too, bristles with vertical pronouns—how different! While the professor points the reader's attention exclusively on the self-important writer, grad-student Abbey makes himself small and dignified while pushing a panoply of "nostalgia buttons" via images that bear a stirring verisimilitude to common human experience and thus strike straight to the hearts of most who read them: Who among us has not at one time and another felt the confusing mix of emotions inherent to recalling love lost?

Restated: Abbey achieves a sublime universality in this passage (as throughout his massive body of work) by describing his personal experiences and feelings in such a way as to trip, in his readers' minds, visceral, virtually palpable recollections of their own similar feelings (if not experiences). He is in fact *creating* nostalgia, thus elevating the art of nonfiction writing beyond literature to the level of heart-to-heart telepathy.

The caper is to keep your focus on the story, the topic, other characters and the needs and desires and knowledge of your *readers*—rather than on yourself. Try to say everything you say about yourself in a way that aids readers in transferring your actions and feelings and opinions and thoughts onto and into *them*selves. In short, *universalize*.

While the professor tells us, in embarrassing detail, about *the professor*, Abbey keeps the focus on Jean—who, due to the common attributes he gives her—becomes a universal lost-love icon, for better and for worse, via his own personal-yet-common and (thus) universalizing memories. The powerful, *sensual* imagines he gives us—of Jean, of the two of them together and the two of them apart—subconsciously plug into our own memories, firing our own emotional recollections. Certainly, *I* can relate; just change the names and I *become* Abbey, awash in bittersweet memory tempered by the retrospective knowledge that subjective loss often prefaces objective gain.

That is great personal writing, worthy of our emulation. In other words:

Regardless of how perfectly a photographer's work renders a subject, it's bound to fail unless it strikes that chord which unloads a common emotional and visual response. (Galen Rowell)

The writer must shed at least a ray of light on human experience, on the human condition. (A. B. Guthrie, Jr.)

All you want in the finished print is the clean statement of the lens, which is yourself, on the subject that has been absorbing your attention. (Wallace Stegner)

The most essential gift for a good writer is a built-in, shock-proof, shit detector. This is the writer's radar and all great writers have had it. (Ernest Hemingway)

The better the book, the more room for the reader. (Holbrook Jackson)

I think the poet articulates the semi-known for the tribe. ... And so a great poet does not express his or her self, he expresses *all* of our selves. (Gary Snyder)

The artist's job? To be a miracle worker: make the blind see, the dull feel, the dead to live. (Edward Abbey)

Stories work on the internal human. Listening to stories is an introspective activity because listeners immediately associate their own experiences with [those] of the story characters. (Susan Strauss)

Certainly, achieving this magical universalizing effect—so widely recognized as being the key to success in all the arts—is easier said than said, yet utterly necessary to strive for.

When speaking in the personal voice—I, me, my, just like the Beatles song—most writers, sooner or later, fall into one of two ego categories: those who are uncomfortable putting their most private selves into their work and therefore avoid first-person at every opportunity, and those who don't seem to know when to turn the spotlight *off* themselves.

That's a generalization, granted, but nonetheless true for a majority of the students I've known in years of teaching, as well as a great many freelancers I've edited. And once, it was true for me as well—the former affliction, that is—a self-conscious hesitancy to embrace Hemingway's "perpendicular pronoun." For many, I suspect this I-me-my phobia is a hangover inflicted by high school composition teachers who graded against expressing "personal opinion" in "theme papers." Even in college, studying "creative" writing, I encountered institutionalized bias against the personal pronoun. "To guard against subjectivity," this anal-retentive mentality seems to reason, "we must go overboard in the other direction."

But that's academe, not the real world of popular publishing. Out here in the sunshine, beyond the ivy-strangled halls of pedantic rigidity, the first-person voice has been creatively and effectively employed for as long as writing has been writ. The key to making the perpendicular pronoun your loyal friend is learning to embrace it—when appropriate—without becoming its slave. Like good whiskey, I-me-my can be addicting and must be tempered with respect for its tendency, if overindulged, to make you feel like Socrates while sounding like Elmer Fudd.

Balance. That's the ticket.

William Strunk and E. B. White, in their venerable *Elements of Style*, advise writers to "place yourself in the background. Write in a way that draws the reader's attention to the sense and substance of the writing, rather than to the mood and temper of the author. If the writing is solid and good, the mood and temper of the writer will eventually be revealed, and not at the expense of the work."

Some writing teachers will profess that Strunk and White are suggesting here a studied avoidance of the first person. I think not. Seems to me they're simply advising us to think hard about *when, where* and *how* we put ourselves into our work. In support of this interpretation, we have White's introduction to *Elements*, the first two sentences of which read:

"At the close of the first World War, when I was a student at Cornell, I took a course called English 8. My professor was William Strunk Jr." That's three personal pronouns in two terse sentences; hardly a studied eschewal of the ownself. But neither do White's references to himself draw undue attention to "the mood and temper of the author": the two perpendiculars are necessary for stage-setting, while the "my" serves as a transition into the subject of this delightful essay— e.g., not White, but his eccentric erstwhile writing professor, William Strunk, and his infamous "little book." Nowhere does White's voice intrude upon the "sense and substance" of his essay. He's simply using what he learned, all those many moons ago, in English 8. And it works.

Similarly, William Zinsser, in *On Writing Well*, appears to offer contradictory advice regarding the first person. In Chapter 4, "Style," he says that "Writing is, after all, a personal transaction between two people. ... Therefore I urge people to write in the first person—to use 'I' and 'me' and 'we' and 'us.'" But then we come to Chapter 21, "Trust Your Material," where Zinsser seemingly swaps ends: "Until recently I felt that the writer should be involved in his story as much as possible. ... But my next book taught me—to my surprise—exactly the opposite lesson. I learned that a writer who intrudes on his material can hurt it badly."

What, exactly, *is* Zinsser saying? Is it thumbs up or down for I-me-my? It's neither. The key word is "intrudes"; think about it. A few pages farther along he amplifies and clarifies: "Maybe you should be strongly present in your story; maybe not—usually the material tells us at the start how it wants to be written."

Just so. Sometimes the vertical magic works, sometimes not. Sometimes we win by placing ourselves prominently in a story, sometimes we lose. And learning to recognize those winning and losing situations really isn't all that difficult—as Zinsser suggests: Just listen to your material.

All of which is well and wonderful, so far as it goes. But in writing, especially nature writing, utilitarian "practicality" rarely takes us all the way. The rest of the trip, and many believe the best part, has to do with matters of the heart and spirit. And of such matters few are more qualified to speak, or can speak more eloquently, than the celebrated author of *Refuge* and *Leap*, Terry Tempest Williams. Years before either of those books came to be, in an unpublished grad-school paper, Terry had this to say about personal writing, providing thus an apropos way to cap and close this chapter:

> I am a naturalist writer. My career and teaching methods have been altered dramatically as a result of my experiences with autobiographical writing. If I am teaching a workshop on creative nonfiction the first exercise I have my students engage in is a "natural autobiography." I ask them to write their personal evolution through their relationship to the natural world. If we are to be writing about landscape, we must be able to reflect on our own sense of place. Through this exercise they are reminded where the source of their power lies—in story, in the Earth and their relationship to life. Simon Ortiz says, "The Earth shall continue as long as the stories and songs continue." I believe if we are to move toward a peaceful future on this planet, it will require each of us to step forward with our own story, trusting the truth of our own experience, to simply tell it straight.
>
> Autobiographical writing introduces us to an ecological model of thinking because we are forced to consider the relationships, to embrace as Gregory Bateson has said, "the pattern that connects." It is this kind of synthesis of personal history and our relationship to the world that creates myth ... the new old story. And it is this realization that propels us out of our own fear of the personal into the collective. Writing has a life of its own. It accesses life, forces the truth. Why does

everyone want to be a writer? Because we crave for expression, for production, for construction of something personal. Ultimately it becomes your personal myth. Mythology is participatory. We have to continue our story.

Optional exercises

Pick a topic you can write about from personal experience and with a true sense of passion—the death or other loss of a loved one, a divorce, a life-changing journey or other significant experience—and spend a thousand words discussing it in first person. Forget about marketability and whether or not what you have to say holds broad interest, and just write this one *for yourself*, as you would in a journal, searching—though never stretching—for epiphany. Cast off shyness. Run emotionally naked and creatively free. No one need see it but you.

When you're finished—comes now the converse—work back through and see how many personal pronouns you can delete—or substitute with the second-person "you"—without weakening or depersonalizing the piece. (Opinions differ, but many modern readers find the impersonal "one" overly formal and distracting, especially in series, which so often seems to accompany its appearance.) You're striving for balance. I regularly employ this drill when self-editing, and it works. (For instance, from the end of the preceding sentence I eliminated a superfluous "for me.")

An even more useful and on-point exercise for first-person writing, if more demanding, would be to emulate Terry Williams' favorite assignment and compose a "natural autobiography" chronicling your personal evolutionary relationship with nature.

Scent Marks in the Snow

Reflections on, and from, a Writer's Ego

Literature consists of those books that make a bid for literary immortality, a length of time that Mark Twain defined as "about thirty to thirty-five years." I'll settle for that. —Edward Abbey

WHILE OUT WALKING MY DOGS one recent wintry day, watching them dash from tree to bush, doing what dogs do, I experienced an unwelcome insight regarding my chosen, and at this point irrevocable, career as a writer. To wit: Nothing I have ever written or am ever likely to write has any more lasting significance than a dog's scent marks in the snow. And I've been brooding about it ever since. After all, I've been a professional writer for half my life—and to what end?

By "professional," I mean merely that I write for a living, freelance and with no financial safety net: no "day" job, no inheritance, no investments portfolio, no drug dealing, no grants, no second income. I've been able to pull it off (marginally and so far) only because I have no dependent children, no mortgage or rent (built my own, very humbly, and paid for it as I went), no expensive habits, no debt, no debilitating fixation on the cultural charade of "financial security" (no health or home insurance and no retirement cache). Best of all, I'm blessed with a wife who, like me, would rather stroll in the woods than a shopping mall.

And it's not so bad. I have all the work I care to do, and most of it meaningful. I have a widely respected literary agent who earns his cut and treats me like a friend in the bargain. I have a dozen books in print and pride in every one, the respect of my peers (those I care about, anyhow) and betters, an intensely loyal (and boundlessly appreciated) if modest readership and, while the antithesis of "rich and famous," I am "making it" as a full-time independent writer—a status that thousands, maybe tens of thousands, of struggling scriveners aspire to without much hope, and which I never really expected to attain myself.

So then, why am I feeling sorry for myself?

Not, I trust, because I worry I've been neglected by the literary "establishment." My gripe is strictly with myself: Water seeks its level, and I fear that I've found mine.

And that's depressing.

Depression, of course, comes with the territory. As does elation. Writing for publication is always a schizophrenic endeavor, an emotional roller-coaster; a high-risk ego sport (ask Brautigan, Hemingway, Kerouac, Woolf). I'm hardly immune, so on bad days I bemoan the probability that I'll always be only what I've always been—a tradesman, never an artist.

Thank the muses that on *good* days I know that the only worthwhile motivations for writing are not public recognition, not money, but having something worthwhile to say and a love of the process of saying it well. Writing's greatest reward—and happily, its most accessible—is its ability to bring some sense and order to the writer's (if not the reader's) little piece of this crazy old world—as evidenced by the fact that so very many "nonwriters" keep careful journals.

Even John Burroughs, the grand old man of nature writing, had to fight the ego blues, counseling himself (and others) that "A man must invest himself near at hand and in common things, and be content with a steady and moderate return if he would know the blessedness of a cheerful heart and the sweetness of a walk over the round Earth." Such "moderate return" should be, and most often must be, reward enough for writing. When I'm down and blue I remind myself of this (as I'm doing even now) and it helps me to regain, and for some time retain, an attitude of gratitude. Which, in turn, is the cornerstone of contentment in life.

Call it career angst. Call it creative crisis. Call it what you will but most problems of writer self-confidence—whether under or over—boil down to *ego*, the archenemy of creativity.

No. Let's try that again: It's the radically *out-of-balance* ego that must be guarded against. Certainly, to the extent that a bedrock belief in the worth of your work is the driving engine of all creative effort, a solid self-confidence is mandatory. As Hemingway once remarked to Charles Scribner: "You have to have confidence to be a champion and that is the only thing I ever wished to be."

Certainly, Hemingway's blue-ribbon self-confidence served him well—at least until that bad Idaho morning when it failed him utterly and he opted for a double-load of buckshot for breakfast. Most cases are less extreme (perhaps because the odds are rarely so high); yet, one way or another, a cocky over-confidence often torpedoes creativity and sends it spiraling out of control all the way to the bottom, down there with the fish poop, forever. As summarized by good, wise old Bud Guthrie: "An absence of confidence is a sure way to a mess. But supreme confidence, the conviction you stand above all suggestions, is just as bad." Worse, I'd say, being far harder to cure. I've seen arrogance and overconfidence doing their cor-rosive work at every level—from first-year college students who already know it all and cockily refuse to learn, to flower-ing literary genius gone to wilt due to the public adoration,

personal and critical insulation and self-complacency attendant to sudden celebrity.

As Barry Lopez—one who has endured literary celebrity for
decades—observes: "Anyone who is writing is writing, in a
sense, out of an extraordinary ego. It's an act of ego ... and it
can be preyed upon by the apparatus for celebrityism in our
culture. So you create this curious situation where a group of
people are writing about something that they understand
fundamentally is larger than themselves, is more important
than themselves—but in order to do it, it is an act of ego. And
then along come the newspapers and other groups of people
who create celebrities and, in some sense, sow contention."

I've seen victims of this "legends in their own minds" dis-
ease, nurtured by a celebrity-hungry media and culture, grow
so smug that nobody is willing, or able should they try, to tell
the emperor he's running around unzipped. A loss to us all.

Happily, there's a sure-fire diet for obese creative egos, albeit
bitter medicine. I know, having swallowed a dose myself some
years ago. In retrospect, I got off easy.

It happened while I was cruising along a New York toll road
in a rental car with a grumpy, seriously hung-over magazine
editor at the wheel; we'll call him Ralph. The year before, I'd
launched a wildlife column for the big national monthly that
employed us both (Ralph in Manhattan, me in Colorado).
Ralph wasn't my boss, but he was politically senior to me, several years older, tight as Siamese clams with the publisher and
a talented essayist who'd once edited a leading natural history
magazine (for which genre I aspired at the time to write). So I
tried to hear what Ralph had to say in spite of the churlish
and abrasive way he had of saying it. Which this day was:
"Those *animal stories* you *crank out* every month—sure, they're
well written, but—*so what?* I mean—what's your *point?*"

I was dumbstruck. And just as well, because I was also mad
as hell. But I sat on my umbrage, as well as my tongue and

fists, and by the time red-eyed Ralph dropped me at the Albany airport for the long flight home, the emotional clouds had lifted and the cold light of truth was beginning to glare through: Ralph was right; in the big picture my "animal stories" *were* pointless. Readers who waded through them would learn some interesting details about the natural world, but that's as far as it went. They were, in effect, shallow natural history; not nature writing. Some essential *something* was missing.

Back home, my ego rudely shaken, as an antidote to despair I revisited some of my favorite writers, nature and otherwise, with an eye to identifying their "points" and how they made them. What I found was a plurality of points, of course, but all wrapped within a single, universal robe: No matter the genre, topic or style, all of the best, most significant and lasting writing—literature, if you will—has the identical bottom line: it sheds some light on the human condition. This holds true for fiction as well as fact.

That was what grumpy old Ralph had tried to tell me in his patently obnoxious way—that my "animal stories" failed the test of literature because they *were* mere animal stories. In writing them, I worked long and hard to describe—with lively anecdote, accurate detail and clarity—the nature of various wild beasts. Yet I consistently failed to go the final yard and connect that wild nature to *human* nature. The moment of that realization—a forced epiphany—marked the beginning of my serious efforts to commit literature. Had I let ego and anger blind me to the truth I was hearing, I'd likely not be writing still today. Thank you, Ralph.

Lesson: Remain open to criticism. And more important, acknowledge and embrace the fact that the most valuable criticism is *critical*. Seek it out. As writers we grow or we wither, and informed criticism is both creative fertilizer and a crash diet for obese egos.

The Ralph incident notwithstanding, obesity of any sort has never been much of a problem for me. Rather, my weakness runs in the other direction; what I need most are safeguards against letting rejection and criticism—my own most especially—suck me down into a whirlpool of depression, creative block and nonproductive despair. One technique I've found to be consistently uplifting is to bear in mind that tastes in writing, as in music, art, whisky and lovers, are wildly subjective. For instance, I find it both heartening and humorous when the same manuscript one editor rejects with scorn, another snaps up with praise; or what one critic sneers at, another applauds. In the end, only *you* can decide which criticisms to take to heart and which to ditch. The tricky bit is doing that sorting with objectivity and without defensiveness.

Yet, it still paints me blue to realize that literary "immortality"—not even Twain and Abbey's tongue-in-cheek thirty to thirty-five years worth postmortem, but merely a few brief shining moments in my own dwindling lifetime—may be forever beyond my clumsy grasp. That's what my dogs reminded me of the other day, and that's what's been chewing on me since. But no more; at least not for a while. After thinking it all through in these meandering paragraphs—striving to put my little acre of life back in order—I can only say: *Petersen, you poor baby. Would you like some cheese with your whine?* Abbey said it all: "There comes a point, in literary objectivity, when the author's self-effacement is hard to distinguish from moral cowardice." Or, as poet and dry–Zen humorist Jim Harrison is wont to advise snivelers, weaklings and malcontents: "Go tell it to Anne Frank."

My agent, bless him, reminded me recently that "it's impossible to prevent periodic emotional downs, but if each time out, you can do a little better than you thought you could, you've won. *That* is the significance of writing, and to my mind, the *only* significance."

Come to think of it, I'd say that's the significance of *life*: doing it the very best you can.

But enough. Time again to whistle up the mutts for a walk. Fresh snow is falling and there's work to be done.

CHAPTER 9

Tense and Person

He ... wanted to write about country so it would be there like Cezanne had done it in painting. You had to do it from inside yourself. ... You could do it if you would fight it out. If you'd lived right with your eyes. —Ernest Hemingway

AMONG THE MOST FUNDAMENTAL stylistic choices you have to make when you first sit down to write are *verb tense* and point of view, also called *person*. In each instance, the choices are but three:

- Past, present or future tense
- First, second or third person

Past tense is far and away the most commonly used in all forms of writing—fiction, creative nonfiction and journalism, even poetry and song. Among its advantages is that readers are accustomed to past tense, and so it doesn't call attention to itself. It's also the most natural for most writers to work with. I can think of no significant disadvantages of past tense, other than, perhaps, its lack of immediacy and the fact that it *is* so commonplace.

Present tense, being less common, does call attention to itself, making it less forgiving all around. For many types of writing it's inappropriate, and for the unpracticed writer it can be tricky to deliver in a natural voice. Advantages of present tense include a heightened sense of tension and, when that's what you're going for, suspense, together with a more urgent, realistic rendering of action scenes, adding up to faster pace and greater reader involvement.

Today, present tense is probably used more commonly in personal narrative, and to better effect, than in any other non-fiction genre. The down-side is that *so* many writers lately are trying to write in present tense, and often doing it so poorly, that some magazines discourage, or even refuse to consider, PT submissions. Even so, I love it, to read as well as to write, and can say why. Calling yet again on Cactus Ed to stand and deliver, here's an excerpt from his early essay "Hallelujah, On the Bum" (in *The Journey Home*), as originally written, in past tense. By way of background, young Ed, having just befriended a kindly old hobo, is about to get his first lesson in train-hopping:

We heard two sharp whistles—the highball signal. Presently the train came slowly through the gloom, three big diesels pulling a string of boxcars so long we couldn't see the caboose. Ponderously the cars rolled by, slowly picking up speed; I could see the wooden ties sinking under the wheels, rising between them. Sealed boxcars passed us bearing brands from all over the nation. … The first empty appeared, doors open; we stood up, stepped into the cinders and gravel of the roadbed, began to trot along beside the train. As the empty came abreast of us, my new friend threw his bundle in, grabbed hold of the edge of the doorway, pulled himself up and half into the car. He turned to give me assistance as I ran along. I was clutching at the edge of the sliding door with one hand, holding my pack and bedroll with the other, reluctant to toss them inside because now I wasn't certain I could get aboard. The floor of the boxcar was chest high and the train was gaining speed. As I hesitated, the old black man grappled me at the wrist with both his big paws and hauled me halfway in; I danced along the ties on tiptoe at twenty miles per hour. "Come on, boy," he hollered, "pitch your roll up and get in here."

Now, the same passage with all the verbs promoted to present tense:

> We hear two sharp whistles—the highball signal. Presently the train comes slowly through the gloom, three big diesels pulling a string of boxcars so long we can't see the caboose. Ponderously the cars roll by, slowly picking up speed: I can see the wooden ties sinking under the wheels, rising between them. Sealed boxcars pass us bearing brands from all over the nation. ... The first empty appears, doors open; we stand up, step into the cinders and gravel of the roadbed, begin to trot along beside the train. As the empty comes abreast of us, my new friend throws his bundle in, grabs hold of the edge of the doorway, pulls himself up and half into the car. He turns to give me assistance as I run along. I clutch at the edge of the sliding door with one hand, holding my pack and bedroll with the other, reluctant to toss them inside because I'm not certain I can get aboard. The floor of the boxcar is chest high and the train is gaining speed. As I hesitate, the old black man grapples me at the wrist with both his big paws and hauls me halfway in; I dance along the ties on tiptoe at twenty miles per hour. "Come on, boy," he hollers, "pitch your roll up and get in here."

Don't know about you, but I find myself reading this second, more urgent and active version, faster than the original, and feeling myself more a part of the action. It's a lesson Abbey quickly learned, coming eventually to embrace present-tense for most of his narrative prose and some of his fiction as well.

Future tense is rarely used, and for reasons good and plenty: it's largely useless other than in dialogue, and even then only for instructing and predicting. Enough said.

Shifting focus now, to person—again, we have three choices: first, second, third. And again, as with tense, only two of the three are broadly useful.

In **first person**—the I-me-my voice—the writer is the narrator, and it's from his or her point of view—mind, eyes, voice, heart, fears and hopes—that the story is experienced and told. Because first person is naturally personal and conversational—like talking to a friend—it facilitates the writer/reader connection. Consequently, it's the voice of choice for nature narration, where the writer is at once observer, participant, commentator, translator and, at the best of times, philosopher.

Though **second person**—you (in the South: "y'all," singular; "all y'all," plural)—has limited application, it's a highly useful tool for inviting readers into the story, into the action, into the written world, and has been used to great effect by such notables as Twain, Abbey and Hemingway. The latter is exemplified in this chapter's opening epigraph, lifted from *The Nick Adams Stories*, slipping smoothly from third to second person and wherein every "you" applies equally to the speaker, "Nick," and the reader, subtly uniting, unifying, universalizing.

While second person is a brilliant tool in limited doses—for instructing, advising, even philosophizing—it tends to sound condescending in narrative, reducing prose to the lowly level of a chamber-of-commerce come-on or real estate ad: "As you top the rise and win your first glimpse of the grand view unfolding below, you feel your heart skip a beat and think to yourself: This is the place!" *Ughh!* (By the way: To whom can one think *other* than to oneself?)

Third person grants the writer/narrator maximum room to move, but keeps her in the shadows, which can be good or bad. In fiction and Hunter Thompson-style "gonzo" or "new" journalism (which relies heavily on traditional fictional techniques), third-person omniscient—"all-seeing" (not to be confused with omnipotent, "all-powerful"), is darn hard to beat. Why? Because you can pass the viewpoint around from character to character. Guthrie employs this technique beautifully in his Pulitzer-winning novel *The Way West*, letting a different character narrate most every chapter, thus providing a refreshingly objective variety of points of view.

In nonfiction, where you can't so easily shift viewpoint or crawl inside other's heads, third person is far more restrictive. Even so, it can be used to good effect in argumentation, explication, description and some narration.

Of course, you're free to mix tense and even person as you will. For instance, I recently edited a story written by a self-described "gnarly mountain chick" who tells of killing a bull elk while hunting alone, and talks intimately about how she came to be a hunter, what nature and hunting mean to her and the special problems and rewards hunting offers a young single woman. Basically, she had written two separate stories— the elk hunt, and a topical memoir. My job as editor was to weave the two together.

Erica opens, *in medias res*, with an ongoing hunt, first person and present tense, taking us skillfully—via scene-setting and description—up to the moment she hears an elk coming and makes ready to shoot. She then flashes back to her childhood—employing a white-space break for transition and shifting appropriately to past tense—up to age sixteen, when she killed her first deer. At this point, via another white-space break, she returns briefly to the elk hunt and present tense, just long enough to remind readers what's going on, further the action and suspense a bit and rekindle interest in the drama's outcome ... then (another space break) resumes her memoir in past tense, bringing it up to date so that the two stories join in present tense, where she concludes and reflects poignantly upon her hunt. Judging from reader response, it worked.

Similarly if far more extensively, in his penultimate novel, *A Fool's Progress*, Abbey breaks creative ground in tense and person manipulation by assuming a third-person narrator's voice to describe present-tense scenes involving the protagonist, one Henry Holyoak Lightcap—while handing the narration over to Henry himself, in past tense, during historical, or "flashback" scenes. It's fun to read, and I'm sure it was fun to write as well, Yet, it proved confusing to many readers and even some literal-minded literary critics.

No matter: As Ed himself liked to say, just do your best and "never apologize, never explain."

Optional exercises

First, study the techniques of several accomplished writers working in present tense, until you have a feel for it. Next, as I did with the excerpt from Abbey's *The Journey Home,* select an active past-tense passage by a good writer and convert all the verbs to present tense.

Now do the same with a piece of your own past-tense prose. Remember, present tense works best in narration, especially where the action is brisk.

With those practice exercises under your suspenders, you should be ready to write something original and splendid in first person, present tense. Next step, should you choose to go there—and applications are largely limited to flashback memories—try mixing past and present tenses in the same piece.

CHAPTER 10

Figuratively Speaking

Do you suppose ... I would put a symbol into anything on purpose? It's hard enough just to make a paragraph.
—Ernest Hemingway

WE HEAR AND USE the term a lot—yet, what *is* "creative" writing? For our purposes here, and for most purposes anywhere, it's writing that allows, facilitates and exhibits the fullest freedom of personal expression. And regarding freedom of personal expression, I perceive five basic levels.

Newspaper-style journalism: "Just the facts, ma'am," with no interjection of the author's personality or views. Third person, past tense.

General nonfiction includes newspaper columns and editorials (which are more personal in outlook and voice than news articles), plus most magazine articles and essays and many books. Here again, third person and past tense are the norm, though the author may, if editorial policy allows, inject his or her own (first person) voice, personality and views.

Poetry: While traditionally aligned with fiction as a creative literary form, poetry is overwhelmingly factual—or, more accurately, reflective. In the words of the great American poet Jim Harrison: "The only source of truth I trust these days is poetry." Aside from its persistent attempts to get at truth, meaning and beauty, the hallmark of poetry is not brevity, not rhyme, but rich, dense, often esoteric figurative language.

Fiction, like poetry, strives to satisfy both the author's goals and the reader's subconscious desires—for entertainment, persuasion, passion, poignancy, tragedy, suspense, surprise, humor, artfulness. Fiction—being an honorable, well-crafted lie—offers the greatest freedom of any form of writing, both technically and expressively.

Creative nonfiction, of which good nature writing is a bright and shining example, employs virtually all of fiction's big box of tricks bar one—it must not lie. The most effective creative nonfiction is, in effect, user-friendly poetry.

In poetry, fiction and creative nonfiction, a variety of devices exist to help the author get across key ideas, images and—most important—feelings, in an easy yet artful manner. Primary among these devices are:

- Allusion
- Symbolism (including Emblems)
- Allegory
- Metaphor
- Simile

Together, these and related devices comprise figurative language.

Allusion depends and calls upon—once or repeatedly—a well-known work of literature, music or visual art. Often, the value of allusion extends no farther than humor, or the subtle self-satisfaction felt by readers who "get it," even though well-wrought allusion is capable of bearing the bulk of a story's premise.

Symbolism involves using something, frequently an object or natural phenomenon, to relate a meaning above and beyond itself. There are two types:

- *Emblems* are universally understood symbols, familiar to all or most readers, at least in your home culture: a country's flag, for an emblematic example, conjures up images and feelings of home, family, patriotism, pride, history—even as the color black universally (in our culture at least) connotes evil and gloom, while white suggests purity and goodness (exemplified in the cowboy movie cliché of black-hatted villains and white-skinned heroes).

• *Symbols* are not universal, but writer-constructed. And they are specific, bearing special meaning only within a particular story, deriving their metaphorical power from context: the dead albatross, for instance, symbolically embodies superstition, shame and pathos (as opposed to classic tragedy) in Coleridge's *Rime of the Ancient Mariner*.

In Matthiessen's *Snow Leopard*, in addition to being a leading character, the unseen cat symbolizes both the wife Peter recently lost to cancer and the elusiveness of meaning in life.

Melville's *Moby Dick* carries unique mystical meaning for each member of the ship's ill-fated crew.

The African river in Conrad's *Heart of Darkness*, along with its copy-cat Cambodian river in *Apocalypse Now*, symbolize spiritual as well as physical journeys.

Abbey's "Moon-Eyed Horse" in *Desert Solitaire*, symbolically embodies the mixed blessings of resolute independence, rebellion and solitude.

And so on. Although it's difficult to construct and employ effective "running" symbols in a brief essay, it's wholly possible; the best writers do it regularly and well. In any and all instances, it's worth noting that literary symbols (including emblems) draw their power from subtlety; symbols can and arguably should be missed by inattentive or unsophisticated readers, thus providing a warmly rewarding feeling of intellectual self-satisfaction for readers alert and savvy enough to sniff them out. Make your symbols too obvious, and they lose much of their potential power.

In review, then, as stated by art scholar Cassandra Langer: "The language of art consists of *emblems* that refer to already existing meanings, and *symbols* that refer only to themselves as originators of meaning."

An **allegory** is a short fictitious story with a moral. Again, there are two types:

• *Parables* feature human characters. For an instance, "The Emperor's New Clothes," which cleverly exposes the pitfalls of hubris and vanity. A longer representative is *Silas Marner*, which explores the suffocating trap of greed.

• *Fables* use animals and/or other nonhuman characters, but anthropomorphize them with such human traits as spoken language, deceit, wisdom and folly.

Of the two, fable has achieved the greater fame because—as with Orwell's *Animal Farm*—it's both fun and meaningful to match human features and personalities with animal traits: pigs are gluttonous and greedy, plow horses are stolid workaholics, owls are professorly, sheep are docile and dumb, foxes are clever but treacherous, milk cows are motherly and so on. Native American mythology, arising as it does from an animistic (zoomorphic) worldview, relies heavily on fable. In Western culture, most of the fable's fame owes to a Greek slave named Aesop and his ingenious moral sketches involving animals. Among my favorites, since it dramatizes my own life choices in a way I find reassuring, is "The Dog and the Wolf":

> Discouraged after an unsuccessful day of hunting, a hungry wolf came upon a well-fed mastiff. The wolf could see that the dog was having a better time of it than he was, and he inquired what the dog had to do to stay so well-fed.
>
> "Very little," said the dog. "Just drive away beggars, guard the house, show fondness to the master, be submissive to the rest of the family and you are well-fed and warmly lodged."

The wolf thought this over carefully. He risked his own life almost daily, had to stay out in the worst of weather and was never assured of his meals. He thought he would try the dog's way of living.

But, as they were going along together, the wolf saw a place around the dog's neck where the dog's hair had worn thin, and asked what this was. The dog said it was nothing, "just the place where my collar and chain rub."

The wolf stopped short. "Chain?" he asked. "You mean you are not free to go where you choose?"

"No," said the dog, "but what does that mean?"

"Much," answered the wolf, as he trotted off. "Much."

A **metaphor** carries an *implied* and *unlikely* comparison (a direct comparison, after all, is nothing but a comparison), or says outright that one thing is something substantially different than what it is. "A good metaphor," observed Aristotle, "implies an intuitive perception of the similarity in dissimilars."

"All the world's a stage, and all the men and women merely players," wrote Shakespeare.

"It is this extraordinary thing, the metaphor," muses Barry Lopez, "that functions in dance, that functions in painting, that functions in sculpture, that functions in literature to allow us to grasp something esoteric in parallel."

The keys are *esoteric, intuitive* and *similarity in dissimilars*. Figurative language in general, and the well-turned metaphor in particular, is the closest we can hope to come to mental telepathy—and at the best of times, as we saw earlier in the bittersweet "Jean" entry from Edward Abbey's journals, plenty close enough—relaying images and feelings far larger and more profound than everyday literal language can handle.

Shakespeare knew this well, and while generally preferring simile, he made great good use of metaphor, as in the following excerpt from the immortal "meeting" scene in *Romeo &*

Juliet, wherein a lust-struck Romeo takes Juliet's virginal hand and the two sweetly rap:

Romeo: If I profane with my unworthiest hand
This holy shrine, the gentle sin is this;
My lips, two blushing pilgrims, ready stand
To smooth that rough touch with a tender kiss.

Juliet: Good pilgrim, you do wrong your hand too much,
Which mannerly devotion shows in this;
For saints have hands that pilgrims' hands do touch,
And palm to palm is holy palmers' kiss.

Romeo: Have not saints lips, and holy palmers too?

Juliet: Ay, pilgrim, lips that they must use in prayer.

Romeo: O, then, dear saint, let lips do what hands do!
They pray; grant thou, lest faith turn to despair.

Juliet: Saints do not move, though grant for prayers' sake.

Romeo: Then move not while my prayer's effect I take.
Thus from my lips, by thine my sin is purged.

[*Romeo kisses Juliet as the stirring orchestral "Theme from Romeo & Juliet" rises to the occasion*]

Juliet: Then have my lips the sin that they have took.

Romeo: Sin from my lips? O trespass sweetly urged!
Give me my sin again.

[*He kisses her again, to the accompaniment of another musical upswelling*]

Juliet: You kiss by th' book.

Oh, be still my lurching libido!

To my eyes, ears and sensibilities, these eighteen lines comprise the finest—most poetic, artful and *moving*—running metaphor ever written, and certainly the most durable; a veritable feast of figurative language. Indeed, no Shakespeare-savvy, spiritually, intellectually and physically vital person watching this scene play out in Franco Zeffirelli's definitive (1968) film rendition can help but feel tears on the cheeks and a stirring in heart and groin. Lordy!

But then, if you haven't had the pleasure of studying Shakespeare and haven't seen the play or movie, you may well feel lost and alone in the maze of Shakespearean doublespeak, as I for so long did. No need to blush. Shakespeare, remember, was not writing books or essays, but stage plays—*visual* literature, in which much of the meaning is translated via facial expression, gesture, body language and staged backdrop. He was also writing in what, to most of us today, seems a foreign tongue, so rife are his works with "low humor," slang and innuendo common in sixteenth and seventeenth century England but never a part of American English, nor, any more, even English English. If you know the lingo, then the deeply, delightfully metaphorical meanings embedded in those eighteen lines from *R&J* are as clear and bracing as glacial ice. But if you're new to Shakespeare, those same lines may as well be writ in Russian. Since it's worth the effort for all writers, in all genres, to unravel a bit of the marvelous, multi-layered figurative language that fairly defines Shakespeare—and thus, to see the invigorating possibilities of metaphorical expression in your own work—we'll give it a go right now.

To begin, these eighteen magical lines complete one English-style sonnet and begin another. Focusing on the final word in each line—*hand, this, stand, kiss/ much, this, touch, kiss/ too, prayer, do, despair/ sake, take, purged, took/ urged, book*—we see the sonnet's rhyme pattern emerge: *ABAB/CBCB/DEDE/FFGH/GH*.

Clever, eh? And *so* boldly subtle that most readers never even notice the rhyme, focusing solely on the romantic action and sexual and social tension. And certainly, rhyme is the least of it. More pertinent to our needs and interests as prose writers is the Bard's luxuriant employment of richly figurative language. Turn with me now to page 867 in our hymnal—*The Complete Pelican Shakespeare*—to those empowering explanatory notes in tiny type at the bottom of each page, where the antique and "foreign" linguistic mystery is interpreted, line-by-line:

"... **94** *shrine* i.e. Juliet's hand; *sin* i.e. roughening her soft hand with his coarser one **95** *pilgrims* (so called because pilgrims visit shrines) **97-100** *Good ... kiss* your touch is not rough, to heal it with a kiss is unnecessary, a handclasp is sufficient greeting **100** *palmers* religious pilgrims **103** *do what hands do* i.e. press each other (in a kiss) **105** *move* take the initiative; *grant* give permission **110** *book* book of etiquette ..."

With these interpretations fresh in mind—quickly! before you forget—revisit the scene and you'll see the religious metaphor that runs (with a delightful touch of heresy, given the strong sexual connotations) throughout; a sweet-flowing river of longing and lust.

All of Shakespeare is thus. If he were easy, everyday, commonplace, so that anyone could comprehend him without effort, then he wouldn't be Shakespeare—and his writing wouldn't make the inimitable magic it does.

Of course, you and I can't write like Shakespeare, and most readers wouldn't want us to if we could. While the Bard shows us the possibilities of figurative language in the grandest cosmic extreme, most prose writers, most of the time, should hover closer to Earth. In others words:

"An imperial crown cannot be one continued diamond: the gems must be held together by some less valuable matter." (Dr. Johnson)

"Too often I encounter men and women, young and old, who speak of the wish to write and the intention of doing so sometime. They populate the meadows of forlorn hopes." (Guthrie)

"I must wonder what will happen when a deteriorating climate, a shrinking food supply, a starving, still-proliferating population and all our varied illusions of central position meet one night on a stormy street corner?" (Robert Ardrey)

"That dog don't hunt." (traditional)

Simile likens one thing to another via words of oblique comparison—specifically, *like, as* and sometimes, *as if.*

"Night fell like a velvet curtain."

"Her tears flowed like wine."

"He's got a heart as big as a whale." (hyperbole)

And what Ray Charles fan does not know and love ...

Your song comes through
As sweet and clear
As moonlight through the pines.

You see it, I trust: the "similarity in dissimilars"? A song cannot, literally, be moonlight—yet, metaphorically, magically, it can.

As per usual, Abbey said it best, in his uniquely playful style, when he quipped that "A simile is like an understanding smile of love—warm, deepening and full of grace."

Herewith a few more examples—each, like Abbey's above, bearing an implicit writing message:

"Every author, however modest, keeps a most outrageous vanity chained like a madman in the padded cell of his breast." (Logan Pearsall Smith)

"A strong wind is not so strong as a wind like a hand in your face. The sun may shine hot, but it shines hotter if it shines hot as a blister or a torch." (Guthrie)

And by way of blending simile and metaphor, this, from Florence R. Shepard:

The life journey toward understanding is like a hike along a trail that encircles a mountain. At each turn a new vista is unveiled. We know that each view reveals a little of what the mountain is. Should we persist to the very summit, we are assured—even there, and by our very experience of this pinnacle—that this too is not *the* mountain. It, like understanding, is not something that can be conquered in one grand assault. Each step of the journey unveils in bits and pieces an authentic approximation of what the mountain really is but can never be known to us absolutely. Our attitude on this journey is one of openness to what lies before us at each step, for each moment contains the consistency and truth of the whole.

By way of brief review:

Love *is* a rose = metaphor

Love is *like* a rose = simile

Which is better? Similes are easier for most writers to invent, and easier for most readers to grasp. Metaphors are more subtle—a gentle brushing of legs beneath a restaurant table—and thus (potentially) more provocative and exciting.

Happily, figurative language is a buffet, not an entrée.

Why bother with working figurative language—symbolism, allegory, metaphor, simile and more—into your writing? After all, writing teachers at every turn advise their students to KISS: Keep It Simple, Stupid.

Why bother? It's the old "picture is worth a thousand words" wisdom. When you compare one thing to another that's substantially different, you create a mental picture that helps translate the essence of your meaning both more effectively, succinctly and with far greater emotional power. Additionally, figurative language helps clarify a particular, less-known thing or idea by comparing it, figuratively, to a general, better-known thing or idea. And best of all, if art is a goal in your writing (and if its not, you're in the wrong game), creatively conceived and wisely employed figurative language can promote your words from paltry prose to proximate poetry.

How so the latter? By providing imaginative mental links that not only paint your message in pretty words, but conjoin the writer and reader's moods and *feelings*. Effective figurative language not only creates images that are more colorful, poetical and thrifty than can be achieved with even the most precise and concrete literal prose—it also evokes, or triggers, universal visceral emotion.

And *that* is the key to the creative universe.

Leonard Bernstein correctly boasted that "music can name the unnamable and communicate the unknowable." Effective metaphorical writing does precisely the same; it *is* music.

Without his genius for figurative language, kept earthy via lots of low humor, Shakespeare would likely have remained a stable boy all his lonely life—or more humbling yet, become an English teacher. Nor can I think of an instance where he over-reached, as you and (especially) I are constantly in danger of doing—say, by attempting to compare two things that are impossibly, even garishly far apart ("The sun was a red wafer pasted against the sky," S. Crane, *Red Badge of Courage*); mixing metaphors ("Out of the frying pan and into the blue"); becoming clichéd, maudlin, gushy, overly dramatic or too prettily purple.

One of the most subtly effective creators of figurative language among contemporary American writers was A. B. Guthrie, Jr. Consider the following snippet of internal dialogue from *The Way West*, delivered through the character of Dick Summers, a kindly, intelligent old mountain man who's deeply saddened by the transmogrifying onrush of civilization and "progress" and sick with nostalgia for the good old days of uninsured freedom and unrestricted adventure:

> A cornfield, even like the sorry patch by the fort, didn't belong with war whoops and scalping knives. It belonged with cabins and women and children playing safe in the sun. It belonged with the dull pleasures, with the fat belly and the dim eye of safety.

"The fat belly and the dim eye of safety." Multitudes spoken in just nine stirringly simple words. And this, from *These Thousand Hills*:

Beyond them, here, just emptiness and open sky. Air like tonic, days like unclaimed gold. And grass and grass and grass.

If you're clever enough, you can purposely abuse figurative language for the sake of humor. But for most of us, it's enough just to use it straight and well "just to make a paragraph." As in most aspects of writing, when in doubt about a figurative device, err toward conservatism.

Optional exercises

Select a piece of prose and read it carefully, as a writer, highlighting and identifying every use of figurative language. And in each instance ask yourself: Does this work, or not? Why so, or why not? How could you make it better?

Now, working with your own writing—a thousand words or so—enhance the piece by inserting at least one well-crafted example of each of the five figurative devices just discussed. Certainly, you'll have to force it a bit—but such is the nature of practice.

Point: Like everything else in writing, after doing it for a while—and after training yourself to recognize it in the work of others—you'll come to a place where context will be your cue to cut a clever figure. Or not.

Go Figure

A Case in Point

As I've said repeatedly and shall repeat again: A big part of a writer's job, especially in the formative phase, is purposeful reading. And not for information only. As you read during the research stage of an article or book project, the part of you that cares about *what* you write is looking for facts, granted. But the part of you that cares about *how* you write should be scanning for such essential elements of style as finely wrought figurative language.

After this fashion and not so long ago, while browsing wildlife magazines at my local public library, I spotted an article about porcupines and, anxious to add to my limited knowledge of these spiny sluggards, gave it a quick read—and in the doing, relearned a valuable writing lesson.

The author—we'll call him Joe—opened with a brief personal anecdote, well done, then went on to outline the natural history of *Erethizon dorsatum* in a clean, interesting, if somewhat formulaic fashion. When I had finished reading, I felt I'd learned a little something about porcupines. And for that I was thankful. Yet Joe wasn't the sort of writer—his style, that is—who motivates me to remember his name and haunt the magazine racks looking for more of his stuff. Lacking comment on the human/nature interface, his work failed to make any memorable points.

Coincidentally, I'd recently (re)read *Jaguars Ripped My Flesh*, an invigorating collection of exceptional magazine features by Tim Cahill. One of my favorite stories in that anthology is "Rime of the Ancient Porcupine," which had appeared originally, some years before, in Tim's long-running "Out There" column in *Outside* magazine. As opposed to Joe's treatment, Cahill's porky story *is* the sort of writing that prompts readers to remember the writer's name and go in search of more.

The point (and lesson) being: Two well-written articles, Joe's and Tim's, both focused ostensibly on the same topic, yet one is eminently memorable and the other easily forgettable. Why?

The answer—beyond the presence or absence of "a point," is *style*. And in this case specifically, *figurative language*. While Joe's article emphasizes information over entertainment, and clarity over stylistic flair—the safe, easy way to go, often preferred by conservative editors—Cahill's is just the opposite. In Tim's essay, the dull nature of the prickly beast is not the true focus—though he does provide several interesting natural facts about porcupines along the way. Rather, Cahill's quill-pig serves as a mirror in which the author reflects eloquently on *human* nature, thus broadening his audience and elevating his efforts to literature.

Briefly, Cahill's "Rime" recalls a time-honored north-country folk belief that the porcupine—like the sailor's albatross—embodies good luck. Reduced to its practical roots, this "good luck" boils down to easy meat. Should you someday find yourself stumbling through a pine forest, lost and starving, a porcupine could save your day. They're plentiful (once you learn where to look for them) and, being mentally and physically sluggish, are easy to approach and kill with stick or stone. And once you get past the prickly bits, the meat is nourishing (if a bit greasy, I'm told). The corollary it follows—according to Cahill, and in parallel with the sailor's superstition regarding the albatross—is that he who wantonly kills a porcupine, without dire need, brings bad luck upon himself and those around him. With this basic background established in a few tight graphs, Tim goes on to tell of a Montana man who, "in the bad winter of 1939," committed the "unholy deed" of murdering a porky that had taken refuge beneath his cabin, disturbing his sleep—and true to legend, paid the price in luck.

You caught the connection immediately, I'm sure, between the title and tilt of Cahill's "Rime of the Ancient Porcupine" and a similar but older tale about a certain aging mariner and an albatross. That connection is neither coincidence nor lowly rip-off, but creative contrivance—*literary allusion* spiced, in this case, with ironic humor. While Joe's piece achieves the writer's ground-floor goal of having something to say and saying it well, Cahill's goes beyond, via figurative language and creative imagery, to stimulate the reader's memory and *imagination* as well. Porcupine as literature.

The essential differences between Joe's and Tim's approaches emerge as early as the titles. While Joe calls his piece (something like) "Porky," Cahill's "Rime of the Ancient Porcupine" surpasses merely identifying the topic and alludes boldly to Coleridge's epic poem *Rime of the Ancient Mariner*—commonly force-read in high school and college lit classes and thus widely known—thereby facilitating the *déjà* view and establishing an eerie, ironic and at once humorous tone for the story that follows.

But just in case, to refresh our memories and include everyone who, like me, dozed through English Lit 101, Cahill clarifies the allusion by reminding us, early on, of the poet's name and voice:

> The ice then, we might conjecture, was here, the ice was there. The ice was all around. It cracked and growled and roared and howled, as Samuel Taylor Coleridge would have it, like noises in a swound.

Having thus set the stage, Cahill leaves Coleridge to his watery pipe dreams and transitions into his own story, tells it, then comes full circle to reconnect with the opening allusion in the closing paragraph:

I like to think that this man, who set a porcupine afire, walked like one that hath been stunned and is of sense forlorn. A sadder and a wiser man, I imagine, he rose the morrow morn.

Allusion, as noted earlier, refers, directly or obliquely, to a well-known poem, book, story, movie, song or what-have-you, and is a mainstay of figurative (also called metaphorical or allegorical) writing. A well-chosen allusion, like the proverbial picture, *is* worth a thousand words. It's better, in fact—richer, more compelling and personal; more movingly memorable. Yet, for all its potential strengths, the considerable skill, effort and knowledge required to employ allusion effectively renders it the least-used major device in the figurative writing arsenal.

Figurative language—allusion, symbolism, allegory, metaphor and simile—doesn't have to be fancy to be effective. One of the most facile discussions I've read on the writer's craft mixes metaphor and simile in comparing an editor to a mechanic and a manuscript to an engine. By employing familiar mechanical terms—honing, adjusting, grinding, tightening, tuning—to summarize how a master mechanic goes about repairing an ailing engine without completely disassembling and rebuilding it with new parts, the writer delivers a telling figurative message about how a good editor repairs only what's wrong with a manuscript without altering its essential character or gratuitously queering the writer's voice with foreign (to the writer's style) words and phrases. And the creator of this mechanical metaphor delivers it in a style that's simultaneously clear, entertaining and memorable. Nothing esoteric, academic or fancy there—just good didactic writing.

No matter how seemingly mundane your topic, a bit of figurative language can add spice to the stew. But here too there be dragons:

- Beware the temptation to over-season, branding yourself an amateur chef (*mea culpa*).
- Beware the metaphorical color purple. Too many writers, reaching too far too fast, get themselves and their readers mired in a bog of overly dramatic figurative speech: "At the roar of the shotgun, the burglar's head exploded like an over-ripe melon hurled down from the heavens by an angry god." (Anonymous, and just as well.)
- Beware the mixed metaphor. As professors Strunk and White caution: "Don't start by calling something a swordfish and end by calling it an hourglass."
- And be aware, in the final count, that not all editors and readers are longing for literary art, figurative or otherwise. And vice versa. I'll bet my skivvies in church that had Joe submitted his "Porky" to *Outside*, it would have come scurrying back (after the usual several months delay), trailing a rejection slip; *Outside* is looking for unique, graceful, high-spirited, mildly "gonzo" writing; not formulaic exposition, no matter how well executed. Similarly, the editorially conservative national wildlife magazine that proudly published Joe's article would likely have rejected Cahill's "Rime" because, sublime as it is, it ain't natural history, and straight-up nature explication, with only minor author involvement at most, is what most non-profit-sponsored wildlife magazines are about.

Research your target magazine before submitting. Who are its readers? Its advertisers? Its editors? What are its politics, preferred style and article length? Then go figure your language accordingly.

CHAPTER 11

Doing It with Style

Discovering Your Literary Voice

Continuous eloquence is tedious.
—Blaise Pascal

"STYLE" IS A WRITER'S distinctive voice. Once you become familiar with a particular style, you'll recognize its author as quickly and surely as you cop to the "Hello" of a friend on the phone or a new song from an old favorite musician after just a couple of notes. While few writers ever develop an award-winning voice, many try—reading, experimenting, attending writer's workshops in search of some magic bullet to individuality. Nonesuch exists. Like maturity and wisdom, style must simply "come." While it can, with work and patience, be encouraged, it can never be rushed, forced or effectively affected.

Speaking to this point, the seventeenth century French philosopher, writer and critic Blaise Pascal quipped that "when we come across a natural style, we are surprised and delighted, for we expected an author, and we find a man." Or a woman, as the case may be.

A good and true writing style—a voice worth singing with in public—is never strained or visibly derivative, but natural, refreshing, original, unique.

A writer's voice or style—the terms are interchangeable—is what sets him or her apart from the pack. Or doesn't. Every serious writer wants a distinctive voice, but few even know what it is, much less how to go about acquiring it. More ironic yet, many writers who *have* a celebrated style can't define its essence or tell you how they came to it. What they can say, however, is that *discovering*—a better word I believe than "developing"—discovering your own style requires first a mastery of the basics of clear, effective communication and composition, the *Elements of Style* stuff, coupled with extensive experimentation, playing around with the possibilities, including, in practice only, consciously imitating the writers whose styles you most admire. Forcing this caper, in college writing classes it's common to have students write a story aping (say) Hemingway's clean, well-lighted voice, then a second, on the same topic, this time imitating Faulkner's eloquently convoluted, difficult style, followed by an open discussion of the differences. Another common—albeit less-challenging and less beneficial—formal exercise is to cursively copy portions of (say again) Hemingway and Faulkner stories, back to back, thus forcing close attention to detail in an effort to hammer home the point that while the two styles could hardly be more divergent, each has merit.

There is no one "best" writing style.

To my sensibilities, the most lyrical stylist writing about nature today is Richard Nelson (who, interestingly, is also a Ph.D. field anthropologist, a subsistence hunter and fisher, and a subarctic surfer). Consider this snippet from Nelson's award-winning memoir *The Island Within:*

> A clear, sharp, whistled voice peals up from the salmonberries. I follow it back along a narrow trail and find its maker: a fox sparrow twenty feet up in an elderberry tree. Wholly engaged in its performance, the bird takes no notice as I ease in below. It looks very plain—reddish-brown on the back, speckled on the breast and sides. Perhaps most of its evolutionary energy went into perfecting this ambrosial song. Every note is like a

beam of brilliant light, woven into a complex, shimmering web. And with each sound, a tiny plume of steam puffs from the sparrow's opened beak, rings and wreathes and curls outward, and dissolves into the crystal morning air. I can almost feel the breath of its song against the bare flesh of my face and fingers. Rich phrases pour down, and the leafless thicket trembles with its own living voice.

Sublime. Yet, looking out through subjective eyes, Nelson belittles his own work while praising that of others. In a recent letter, for instance, he humbly defers to a 1967 book I'd not previously heard of, *The Peregrine*, by an English writer I had not previously known, John A. Baker. "Baker's writing," says Nelson, "is the most intense, powerful and evocative I have come across. I keep *The Peregrine* next to my desk and to get my juices flowing I read passages before I start to write. These little readings are not entirely good for me, though, because the incredible richness of Baker's language is so humbling. The book is organized like a journal, and the passage I love best is for February 10, describing a peregrine's stoop." Here is the terminal portion of that passage:

For a thousand feet he fell, and curved, and slowly turned, and tilted upright. Then his speed increased, and he dropped vertically down. He had another thousand feet to fall, but now he fell sheer, shimmering down through dazzling sunlight, heart-shaped, like a heart in flames. He became smaller and darker, diving down from the sun. The partridge in the snow beneath looked up at the black heart dilating down upon him, and heard a hiss of wings rising to a roar. In ten seconds the hawk was down, and the whole splendid fabric, the arched reredos and immense fan-vaulting of his flight, was consumed and lost in the fiery maelstrom of the sky.

And for the partridge there was the sun suddenly shut out, the foul flailing blackness spreading wings above, the roar ceasing,

the blazing knives driving in, the terrible white face descending—
hooked and masked and horned and staring-eyed. And then
the back-breaking agony beginning, and snow scattering from
scuffling feet, and snow filling the bill's wide silent scream, till
the merciful needle of the hawk's beak notched in the straining
neck and jerked the shuddering life away.

And for the hawk, resting now on the soft flaccid bulk of his
prey, there was the rip and tear of choking feathers, and hot
blood dripping from the hook of the beak, and rage dying
slowly to a small hard core within.

"Intense, powerful and evocative" indeed—but so is Nelson's
work. And where Baker often ignores Pascal's caution against
the tediousness of "continuous eloquence," Nelson never does.
As with Hemingway and Faulkner, one is "better" than the
other only when viewed through subjective preference. Therefore, I repeat: While there are weaker and stronger voices, there
is no one "best" style, since literary beauty lives, indeed and in
fact, in the eye of each beholder, and variety is the spice.

With the basics of composition tucked firmly under your cap,
with experimentation and imitation and practice and objective self-criticism and persistence and *luck*, you'll eventually
discover, acquire, find, develop, a personal voice that fuses
stylistic elements of the various writer's you've studied
(which should be your own favorites, not those suggested by
some "expert"), together with something fresh and utterly
original. At that happy juncture, your writing is no longer
imitative of your exemplars, but will be said by knowing
readers and reviewers to be "influenced by" so-and-so. You'll
have transcended experimental emulation to arrive at a personal voice that comes easily and naturally and is adaptable
to any writing situation.

At least that's the hope. That's the goal. That's the plan.

One effective way to study style is to learn not only to "hear" or discern different voices when you encounter them, but to understand what *makes* them different, one from another, for better and for worse. Here are some points to consider:

- Why is one word used when another, perhaps more common or simpler word would serve? Is the writer merely flaunting the fact that she owns a thesaurus—or is she going for the distinctive sound, rhythm or subtle meaning of the unaccustomed word?

- Is there an identifiable pattern to the way sentences are put together? Paragraphs? Essays?

- How are transitions handled?

- Is there a pattern of unusual punctuation—purposeful sentence fragments, intentional "run-on" sentences, lots of long or short sentences or graphs, omission of commas in a series, lots of parentheticals, modifiers, etc.?

- Tune in to phrasing, idiom and other distinctive ways of speaking. While a Limey, an Aussie and a Yank ostensibly speak and write the same English, the discerning ear can, within the first few syllables, tell which from whom and where.

- Is a style notably formal, distinctly informal or somewhere in between? Does the level of formality alter from work to work, and if so, how and why do you suppose?

- How does the writer use cadence—the speed at which the style of delivery leads you to read? For example: A rapid-fire series of short, sparse sentences constructed of crisp, unmodified nouns and active verbs can build excitement and a sense of urgency that prompts you, quite subconsciously, to read faster ... while big words and long, modifier-laden sentences slow your reading and moderate your mood. Which is not to say that short is preferable to long or simple to complex. An experienced writer knows the differences and uses them in variety to consciously influence the reading pace and mood:

faster and simpler for action and suspense, slower and more involved to create a reflective or somber ambience.

Another common element of style is *rhythm*. Rhythm in writing is the calculated organization of syllables, words, even sentences, into a pattern that musically pleases the ear without overtly rhyming. Important elements of stylistic rhythm you should endeavor first to recognize in the work of others, then to internalize in your own writing, include:

Vocabulary: Extensive or sparse, stiff or relaxed? Smooth and natural or awkward and forced? Melodic or dissonant?

On the topic of vocabulary, Bud Guthrie snaps that "What using long words proves is that the author has some acquaintance with some long words." Not even that, necessarily, if she or he owns a thesaurus.

Moreover, "an acquaintance with some long words" isn't necessarily bad. There's a time and a place for (almost) everything. Having learned long ago the importance, so far as possible, of tailoring voice to audience, I automatically mold my vocabulary to fit my image of the "target" readers of a particular magazine or book. Even so, a style is a style and there's always a certain sameness to it. In my case, I like to spice a relaxed, personal, "down home" voice with the occasional magnanimous mouthful of vocabulary or thought. The only real variation is in the relative size of the portions. If nothing else it's fun, and gives critics something to criticize.

Alliteration involves stringing together words whose dominant syllables, being usually but not always the lead syllables, have similar sounds yet rarely rhyme. For instance, the last five words of the previous sentence. Or, as in Shakespeare's *Macbeth*: "We met them, daring, beard to beard, and beat them backward home."

I am, as you are by now no doubt aware, a raving alliteration junkie. Although I know well its dangers, I find the urge to play this way almost irresistible. The more alliteration you see in my "stuff," the more fun you can know I'm having. Of course, fun or not, it's whether it *works* or not that counts. Because it's so very obvious, you can easily overdo alliteration, and often I worry that I do. But—like good puns, good single-malt and good love (not at all in that order)—I find alliteration far too compelling to fully forego. And at least a few readers, it seems—sharing my love of low humor—rather like it. Yet, while it's too late for me, I counsel alliterative restraint on your part.

Asyndeton is the replacement of conjunctions with commas to achieve a sense of compression, speed and certainty—like Caesar's boast after crushing Gaul: "I came, I saw, I conquered."

Or Lincoln's Gettysburg sound bite: "Of the people, by the people, for the people."

Both of which also exemplify …

Parallelism—being the expression of co-ordinate ideas in similar rhythmic form, as in this poetically prophetic example from *Leap*, Terry Tempest Williams' artful memoir:

> The restoration of nature, even our own, will require a reversal
>   of our senses and sensibilities.
> To see with our heart.
> To touch with our mind.
> To smell with our hands.
> To taste with our eyes.
> To hear with the soles of our feet.

In those five infinitive lines of parallelism, Terry also demonstrates two more stylistic techniques:

Single-sentence paragraphs for power and punch, and …

Cross-over sensory images, which, in turn, are closely related to what Guthrie dubs …

Misplaced modifiers. "What might be called the misplaced modifier," Bud explains, "is an effective tool for novelty. I wrote once of 'the breathless upthrust' of the Grand Tetons. The Tetons aren't breathless; the onlooker is. One sense can be employed to strengthen and enlarge the force of another. ... Sound for sight, and sight all the better for it."

True enough, as in Abbey's classic *Desert Solitaire* image: "The sun roared down from its place in Heaven."

Oxymoronic juxtaposition is a close confederate of both cross-over imagery and misplaced modifiers, matching as it does two words or phrases that, literally interpreted, tug in opposite directions, but when joined produce a surprisingly compelling image:

The Perfect Storm

The Nearby Faraway

"Her parting kiss was the cruelest kindness."

"His violent reaction revealed an awful innocence."

"A terrible beauty is born." (Yeats)

And of course the iconic oxymoronic cliché: "military intelligence."

Polysyndeton is the adverse of asyndeton, involving the replacement of commas with conjunctions to achieve a pulsating, undulant rhythm:

"As they sped along the mountain road, the horizon narrowed and widened and rose and fell."

Personification attributes human characteristics, often emotions, to the nonhuman world:

"The ocean sleeps today."

"The sky was angry."

Humor is damn good work if you can get it. "Anywhere, anytime," says Abbey quite seriously, "I'd sacrifice the finest nuance for a laugh, the most elegant trope for a smile." That was Abbey's style, as it is also Tim Cahill's, John Nichols', Hunter Thompson's and other writers I and thousands more admire. Why? Because there's never enough laughter in the world. If you can elicit even one good chuckle in the course of an essay, readers will remember that essay, and its author, with grateful favor. And too, as Abbey knew, if you can sweeten bitter medicine—which most environmental writing tragically is—with an occasional grin or guffaw, it's a whole lot easier to swallow. This philosophy allowed Abbey, single-handedly, to convert more readers to nature-love and recruit more eco-warriors than all the hard-biting "environmental literature" ever written. I know, being one of both of them.

But for all its laudable qualities, humor can no more be forced than can style. Like physical attractiveness, we *largely* either have it—a gift—or we don't. Yet happily, this is not *wholly* so. Studying the techniques of successful humorists is a viable way to approach a humorous style of your own. John Nichols, for example, frequently sets readers up for a laugh by popping his funnies when they're least expected—smack in the middle of a serious discussion—capitalizing on the element of surprise.

Purposeful ambiguity has nothing to do with muddy writing. Rather, it's the high-end literary art of stopping enticingly short; dropping hints; leaving a little something to the reader's imagination; a teasing nightie compared to raw nudity. Among the finest (classiest and most colorful) examples of purposeful ambiguity emerges as the denouement in what many consider Hemingway's finest moment, an African tale called "The Short Happy Life of Francis Macomber." As retold by Guthrie in *A Field Guide to Writing Fiction* (a slender classic, regretfully allowed to fall out of print but worth tracking down):

> Macomber, shamed for having fled before the charge of a lion, later finds courage and stands resolute as a swamp buffalo charges him. His wife, behind him, fires her rifle, maybe at the buffalo, and by accident or design shoots Macomber in the back of the head. The force of the bullet knocks him face

down. The wife and the white hunter run to the body. Here the amateur writer would have had a great time describing what a mess of head and face the bullet made on emerging. Instead, Hemingway has the white hunter say, "I wouldn't turn him over." What a spur to the reader! His imagination takes wing. He doesn't need imprisoning words. His imagination soars above all the adjectives and enforcing phrases of verbal resources.

Further, if you're *reading as a writer*, you'll have noted that Guthrie's subtly intriguing description of Mrs. Macomber's aiming and firing "maybe at the buffalo … by accident or design," is itself a clever bit of ambiguity. "Which was it," we're left to wonder: "Accident or design"?

There are styles, and there are styles. What is it that makes one writer's voice unique, pleasing, memorable, compelling, even magical—while so many others are remarkable only in their glaring unremarkability? In part, it's a combination of all the above devices, and more—with much of that "more" referring to not just *how* a writer writes and which tools she chooses to use, but what she has to *say* and with what degree of honesty and passion she says it.

Additionally:

Watch out for loose descriptions, abstractions, words of large embrace. What does "beauty" mean or "beautiful" or "terrible" or "tragedy" or "ecstasy" or "magnificent"? Something, to be sure, and much sometimes. But illustrations and specifics are surer aids to ends. (Guthrie)

"Too many words" is [Doug] Peacock's [*Grizzly Years*] chief complaint about writing. Peacock believes that if the story is good, a writer doesn't need many words to tell it, just a few to guide readers along, lodestars to keep them on the trail.

Landmarks or cairns. Points of reference. If the story has been told too much, the path becomes worn and boring. So some writers use more and fancier words to confuse readers into believing that the story they are reading is unique. Also, it seems, too many writers are so seduced by their own words that they forget the story, forget they need a story. (Brooke Williams, *Halflives*)

Style: There is something in too much verbal felicity that can betray the writer into technique for the sake of technique. (Abbey)

The art of art, the glory of expression and the sunshine of the light of letters, is simplicity. (Walt Whitman)

A poem is just a statement and not a song, unless it's got language expressing through sound what is going on. (Galway Kinnell)

Go back and look at your writing in relation to its sound and sense, to see whether the sounds are reinforcing the meaning. (Barry Lopez)

If it is not in the teller's imagination and soul, it will not enter the audience's. (Susan Strauss)

Utterly optional exercise

The names of the foregoing stylistic techniques are not in themselves important, other than as hooks from which to hang our understanding of the writing techniques they identify—which, come to think of it, is quite important. Were I you, I would memorize them all—or make a "cheat sheet" of names and brief definitions on the back of a (big) bookmark. Then, next time you read a book or essay and forever after, recall a device's name and review its uses. Who knows—you may even spot some of the above tools embedded, heretofore anonymously, in your own evolving style.

Try them all, every last one, again and again, until you feel wholly comfortable with their lurking companionship. Then, as with almost all didactic formalities of writing and style— put them out of your conscious mind. At that point—when, say, an alliteration appears in your prose—you'll know that it's honest and natural, never contrived or tedious. As Annie Dillard remarks in *Living by Fiction*: "One does not produce a work and then give it a [stylistic] twist by inserting devices and techniques here and there like acupuncture needles."

Well—some "ones" sometimes do.

CHAPTER 12

Filthy Dirty Grammar

(An Excuse to Review Two Good Books)

Huh?
—traditional

AFTER STUDYING GRAMMAR for three decades and struggling to teach it for one (in college "advanced comp" classes, which, from my jaded experience at a Colorado "ski school," could just as well be called "kindergarten komposition"), I'd rather not even talk about it. Not here, anyhow. Not now. Not in this otherwise sweet, happy, intimate, mature and easy-going tome.

We don't *need* no stinking grammar, you and me.

But in truth, of course we do. It is in fact of paramount importance to successful writing, no matter how we define "success." Stephen Topping—my amiable editor at Johnson Books, with years of New York "big house" experience, recently remarked: "While learning my craft as editor I also learned a lot about grammar. Now, I judge the professionalism of a writer by the lack of common errors. A writer's level of craftsmanship is very much a part of my decision to publish or not." As it is with virtually all literate editors.

Grammar—comprising, among other skeletal elements of clear communication, what we call "mechanics"—is nothing less than essential.

Yet, my point and inclination are: This is not the book, and I am not the guy, to dish out that bitter bowl of beans. The guys for that job—the Grammar Guys—are the nefarious and aforementioned duo of William Strunk Jr. and Elwyn B. White, author and editor, respectively, of the inimitable, indispensable *The Elements of Style*. This minuscule masterpiece, comprising just eighty-five pages, is a rare good bargain in today's grossly inflated academic book market and a godsend for all serious writers, editors and composition teachers. I own three copies of *Elements* (though I'm not sure why) and reread one or another of them, cover to cover, once a year at least; it takes but one languid winter's eve. In the shameful and disabling event you're as yet unfamiliar with this little classic, and in place of a grammar lesson from me, here's a quick preview.

The original, self-published *Elements of Style* was written more than eighty years ago by Cornell University English professor William Strunk Jr., whose goal, says former student White in his (aforementioned) introduction, was "to cut the vast tangle of English rhetoric down to size and write its rules and principles on the head of a pin." Indeed, in his merciless "cutting down," Strunk reduced the whole bloated business to a mere "Seven rules of usage, eleven principles of composition, a few matters of form, and a list of words and expressions commonly misused. … *The Elements of Style* does not pretend to survey the whole field. Rather it proposes to give in brief space the principal requirements of plain English style. It concentrates on fundamentals: the rules of usage and principles of composition most commonly violated."

And therein lies the tenacious charm and unique utility of the tiny tome known to grateful writers worldwide simply as "Strunk & White." Let's sample a taste from each of its five parts.

Part I — Elementary Rules of Usage

"Enclose parenthetic expressions between commas."

One of the great strengths of *Elements* is its clear and abundant examples—for example, regarding the above rule:

"The best way to see a country, unless you are pressed for time, is to travel on foot."

Thus, even if you're confused by the grammatical jargon—which the authors attempt to keep a leash on but occasionally let run wild—simply by studying the examples you'll still catch the pass. And once you've got the ball in hand, you can run with it sans the academic lingo. Beyond that and remarkably, after explaining the rule, S&W often go on to advise us of exceptions, as well as if, when and how the rule can be creatively broken.

Part II — Elementary Principles of Composition

"Choose a suitable design and hold to it.

"A basic structural design underlies every kind of writing. The writer will in part follow this design, in part deviate from it, according to his skill, his needs, and the unexpected events that accompany the act of composition. Writing, to be effective, must follow closely the thoughts of the writer, but not necessarily in the order in which those thoughts occur. This calls for a scheme of procedure. In some cases the best design is no design, as with a love letter, which is simply an outpouring, or with a casual essay, which is a ramble. But in most cases planning must be a deliberate prelude to writing. The first principle of composition, therefore, is to foresee or determine the shape of what is to come and pursue that shape."

Here I dare to quibble: To be most effective, a love letter should *not* be "simply an outpouring," which risks incoherence, slop and inadvertent hurtfulness, but a *thoughtful* and *carefully crafted* outpouring. Similarly, even a "casually rambling" essay, to work, needs plan and purpose.

Part III — A Few Matters of Form

"*Colloquialisms*. If you use a colloquialism or a slang word or phrase, simply use it; do not draw attention to it by enclosing it in quotation marks. To do so is to put on airs, as though you were inviting the reader to join you in a select society of those who know better."

Part IV — Words and Expressions Commonly Misused

"*Nauseous. Nauseated.* The first means 'sickening to contemplate'; the second means 'sick at the stomach.' Do not, therefore, say 'I feel nauseous,' unless you are sure you have that effect on others."

What? Stuffy old English professors with a sense of humor?

Part V — An Approach to Style (With a List of Reminders)

"*Write with nouns and verbs* ... not with adjectives and adverbs. The adjective hasn't been built that can pull a weak or inaccurate noun out of a tight place."

Although this sampling is necessarily sparse (there are, after all, copyright laws to honor), you may have seen enough to note that *Elements* is organized, logically, with the most elementary—and thus the most "grammatical," thus most boring and potentially confusing—material up front, moving along through increasingly advanced advice to finish with some right nice stylistic tips.

And so it is that anytime anyone hits me with something like "I have some things to say and I want to become a writer. Where should I begin?" I suggest they buy and study Strunk & White. If I see them later and they have done so, I know they're serious. If, however, they "haven't had a chance" to read *Elements*, yet continue to gush about "wanting to write," I smile and turn away. It's that elemental.

After graduating yourself from the University of Strunk & White, the next step toward internalizing the essential rules—and the last such step you'll likely ever need to take—is to buy, study and freely consult the bible (in that it lays down the laws) of professional writing and editing: *The Chicago Manual of Style*. This too we shall briefly review. But first, a bit of background.

I came to professional writing by happy accident and rather late in life, and without ever having suffered an urge to "express myself" in print. (Spontaneous side note regarding revision, self-editing and ego: I just spent an hour writing a detailed chronology of my life up to and through the point of going freelance some twenty years ago, thinking it an appropriate way to introduce my next point—then, in instant retrospect—Hemingway's "internal B.S. alarm" screaming—recognized the whole works as superfluous if not self-indulgent, and trashed it all. Good on me. And good on you when you do the same. I think it was southwestern writer Frank Waters who offered the ruthlessly practical writing advice to "Murder your darlings." Similarly, Hemingway said something like "You can tell the worth of a writer by how much he can afford to leave out." And long before either of those two, Sam Johnson noted that "An old tutor of a college said to one of his pupils: Read over your compositions, and wherever you meet with a passage which you think is particularly fine, strike it out.") Rather than feeling driven to write, I came to writing through editing, and got into editing by accident.

Thus I learned, up-front and first-hand, that most editors are overworked and underpaid and so will often accept relatively uninspired but mechanically clean submissions—those that require little of the editor's precious time or energy—while often rejecting brilliant but sloppy manuscripts requiring significant editorial labor. So it was, right from the start, I determined to fine-tune all my manuscripts to the point that little if any further mechanical adjustment was necessary. It worked. Still does. Editors love writers who save them time. I try to do my part to comply, and if you want to sell what you write, so will you. Besides, having your squeaky-clean manuscripts only lightly edited, if at all, is—well, gratifying.

But in order to submit grammatically and mechanically clean manuscripts we must know the rules, both basic and specific. The basics are all right there in Strunk & White. For the specifics, you'll need to cozy-up to *The Chicago Manual of Style*. It's *such* a standard reference that anytime I encounter an editor who *doesn't* rely on *Chicago* (which is almost never), I know I'm toying with a loose cannon. (Beware: Newspapers have their own, specialized publishing guide, the *Associated Press Style Book & Libel Manual*. It is *not* a substitute for *Chicago*.)

In exact opposition to *Elements, Chicago* is a big—921 pages, weighing several pounds—complex and fairly expensive volume. But you *need* it, and unlike *Writer's Market* (more about that later), which is updated annually, one *Chicago* should last a writing lifetime. By way of previewing this hefty helper, we'll simply scan the Contents pages, introducing three parts and nineteen chapters, plus extensive front- and back-matter. (Don't know the terms "front-matter" and "back-matter"? *Chicago* will fill you in.)

Contents
Preface
Part 1 — Bookmaking
   1 The Parts of a Book
   2 Manuscript Preparation and Copyediting
   3 Proofs
   4 Rights and Permissions

Part 2 — Style

Part 3 — Production and Printing

There's virtually *nothing* of professional importance on the topics of writing, manuscript preparation, editing and producing books and magazine articles—including rights, permissions and other pertinent peripherals—that isn't covered in *The Chicago Manual of Style.*

Granted, most magazines and book publishers have their own "house styles." For instance: Little, Brown and Company sends its contracted writers a neatly bound, fifty-eight-page style guide exuberantly titled *From Manuscript to Printed Book: Exhortations and advice to our authors for preparing manuscripts for the press.* At the opposite extreme, all "together" publishers offer at least a couple of photocopied pages of specific stylistic advice—after all, it benefits no one more than the editors. Yet, most such guides merely reflect that particular house's preferences within the parameters set by *Chicago*. For instance, the above-mentioned Little, Brown guide includes the proviso: "For complexities of style not covered by this booklet, *The Chicago Manual of Style* is our primary authority."

Without the universal standard so well provided by *Chicago*, the publishing industry would soon degenerate into stylistic anarchy. *So* deeply embedded is *Chicago* in the editorial psyche that if someday you find yourself entangled in a friendly argument with an editor over some stylistic difference, no matter how esoteric, the first one to finger chapter and verse in *Chicago* in support of her point, wins.

Mandatory exercise

This time you have no option. If you want to succeed as a writer—"nature" or otherwise—you simply must buy and study *The Chicago Manual of Style* and *The Elements of Style*, neither of which contains practice exercises.

(Author's note to Macmillan Publishing and The University of Chicago Press: Please remit payola checks promptly.)

INSTRUCTIVE INTERLUDE

A College Writing Short-Course
(With lots of help from Mark Coburn)

HOW MANY WRITERS have you known who enjoy, honestly *enjoy*, dealing with the cranky trio of grammar, punctuation and syntax? Between (and including) us, we know not a one. But enjoyable or not, the immutable rub is that mastering these bothersome technical details is essential—not just to good writing—but to selling what you write and otherwise being perceived as a professional.

In our overlapping roles as writers (two), editor (one) and college English professors (1.5), we have, over the years, noticed the same six grammatical errors popping up with the frequency and tenacity of adolescent acne—not just in student essays, but in far too many articles and book manuscripts penned for publication by "real" writers. As a cure for these nagging grammatical ailments we offer herewith a six-dose prescription.

1. Apostrophe errors: The most common apostrophe error is to confuse *its* with *it's*. The former, minus apostrophe, is the possessive form; the latter, with apostrophe, is a contraction for "it is." Correct: "The deer flicked its tail." "It's a lovely deer." Other pronouns not taking an apostrophe in the possessive form are hers, theirs, yours, ours and whose.

2. Subject/verb disagreement: This error is particularly easy to make when a word or phrase intervenes between a verb and its subject. Incorrect: "The power of romantic love—its fears, hopes and roller-coaster ups and downs—*are* not easily ignored." Remember: The word or phrase governing the verb doesn't

139

necessarily immediately precede the governed verb. To eliminate the confusion, mentally eliminate the intervening phrase. Correct: "The power of romantic love ... *is* not easily ignored."

3. Pronoun disagreement: Watch for singular pronouns that pose as plurals. Particularly troublesome are "everyone" and "everybody." Incorrect: "Everybody who applies for this job is going to have *their* references checked." Correct: "Everybody (or everyone) who applies for this job is going to have *his* references checked." (If "his" carries too strong a sexist odor for you, then recast the sentence in the plural: "All those applying for this job will have *their* references checked.")

In a related matter, the noun "none" takes a singular verb when its meaning is "not a single one." Correct: "None of the animals *has* rabies." However, when "none" is used to suggest more than one, it takes a plural verb. Correct: "None *are* guiltless save those as yet unborn."

4. Tense disagreement: With rare exception, the rule is to keep to one tense per sentence, and preferably per paragraph. If you begin a paragraph in the past tense—"In one of his most grueling adventures, mountain-man John Colter *trudged* five hundred miles, alone, through the winter wilderness"— don't end it in present tense—"After surviving all those hardships, Colter eventually *returns* to the fort and safety." The place to change tenses (and then never capriciously) is at the beginning of a new paragraph, or, better yet, after a whitespace ("silent transition") break.

5. Sentence fragments: To be grammatically correct, a sentence must contain a subject (noun or pronoun) and a predicate (verb or verb form) and make sense on its own. To understand this concept completely, it helps to be able to distinguish between a phrase, a dependent (also called subordinate) clause and an independent (also called main) clause, to wit:

A *phrase* is a group of words lacking either subject or predicate, or both.

A *dependent clause* contains both subject and predicate, but relies on the remainder of the sentence to clarify its meaning.

An *independent clause* contains both subject and predicate and can stand alone in meaning; it is, in effect, a simple sentence.

"Jumping aside, he dodged the falling rock." In this example, "Jumping aside," since it contains no subject, is a phrase—while "he dodged the rock" is an independent clause; it has both subject ("he") and predicate ("dodged") and could stand on its own as a simple sentence.

"After they finished dinner, they went for a hike." In the first part of this example, the pronoun "they" is the subject, while "finished" is the predicate—yet the clause "After they finished dinner" has no meaning on its own, but is *dependent* on the second clause.

The point of all this? To avoid writing sentence fragments, be certain that each of your sentences contains at least one independent clause.

Creative exceptions: Occasionally, you may wish to employ an intentional sentence fragment in order to gain a particular effect—as with the question we used to open the preceding paragraph. Additionally, it's perfectly acceptable (even necessary) for written dialogue to reflect the fact that people frequently speak in sentence fragments:

"Why not?" Otis demanded to know.

"Just because," Roxanne fired back.

6. Comma splices involve the incorrect substitution of a comma for a period, colon, semicolon or em-dash. Incorrect: "This morning I was late for class, Petersen was already running his big mouth when I got there, he talks so much and says so little." The simplest (though not the only) fix here, short of tossing Petersen off campus forever, is to divide the run-on statement into three separate sentences, replacing the commas with periods.

To balance those six negatives, here are half-a-dozen positive writing tips:

1. Don't be a bore. What is boring? Dragging out an obvious point, using the same words repeatedly, writing each sentence the same way—these are a few of the most common yawn-makers. Additionally, the excessive use of words and phrases we have all heard too often can for sure be a major factor in boring a reader. Consider our use of "for sure" and "major factor" in the preceding sentence. The former is empty slang, while the latter is starchy and officious; both are worn-out, boring phrases. Avoid them and all their windy ken.

2. Remember that the reader is not you. Have you ever tried to assemble or learn to use something (for a pertinent instance, a word processor) from lousy directions? That's a common example of writing that fails because the writer did not put himself in the reader's place. Organization, clarity and completeness—these are the keys to making yourself understood.

3. Use strong verbs. Dull writers employ dull verbs, then try to make up the difference by glopping on gaudy adverbs and adjectives. Example: "Punting was the key factor in the home team's win." Find a livelier verb than "was" ("gained," "netted," "earned," etc.) and you'll never need vacant, modifier-ridden phrases like "key factor" or "major element." Another example: "She moved quickly along the hiking trail." Why use the imprecise verb "moved," weighted with the adverb "quickly," when you can get the job done more economically and efficiently with a single precision verb—such as "hurried" or "scurried"?

4. Put punch in your sentences by embracing the active voice and shunning the passive. Passive: "The annoying little kid was eaten by the angry bear." Active: "The angry bear ate the annoying little kid." Watch for such passive tip-offs as "was" and "were."

5. Vary the strength, length and form of your sentences and paragraphs. For instance, give readers a brief mental break by following an exceptionally long graph with a one-liner. And why not ask an occasional question? But don't overwork exclamation points! Save them for true exclamations: "Ouch!" Mix things up. Keep it lively and modestly unpredictable.

6. Be suspicious of abstractions. Use sharp details to nail down your points. Consider the following sentence-pair by a black militant: "I don't want white Americans to love me in Christian brotherhood. I want them to stop bombing little girls in churches and beating me with clubs." Notice how flabby and phony the abstractions of the first sentence of this example (ours) look alongside the explicit details of the example sentences.

Most people, writers included, are not wildly original thinkers. Little is new under the sun (including that old cliché); your ideas have probably been voiced, in so many words, many times before. Consequently, particularly in nonfiction, it often isn't so much *what* you say as *how* you say it that determines the perceived worth of your writing. With attention to detail and tireless practice, your prose can be as distinctive as your footprints in the sand. Make your writing express you at your best; make it as precise as you can make it; and keep it lively.

Readers today—magazine and book editors included—must wade through so *much* verbal mud; imagine how grateful they'll be when you provide them with clear, grammatically correct manuscripts that are crisp, original and a pleasure to read.

CHAPTER 13

Re-vision

Where the Real Writing Begins ... and Ends

The [writing] *game is won or lost on hundreds of small battles.*
—William Zinsser

TO ZINSSER'S EPIGRAM I would add, and emphasize, that most of those battles, small and otherwise, are fought on the field of revision. In fact, were I asked for a one-word definition of the writing process, that word would be "rewriting." Or, more revealingly, "re-vision."

"In the beginning was the Word. And the Word was *revise*."

Self-editing follows precisely the same rules as editing others, yet is infinitely more challenging because of ego interference and lack of objectivity gained through critical distance—even as we're often unaware of our own body odor or coffin-breath, but can smell them in others a mile away. And just as troublesome, writers, being a delicate lot, are often overly critical of themselves, to the point of replacing self-confidence with paranoia and creative suffocation. At the worst of times, to paraphrase Simone Beauvoir, would-be writers are "filled with such horror at the idea of a defeat that they keep themselves from ever doing anything."

In my early years of writing professionally, I was rigidly structured regarding revision, to the point that it was tractor-slow, gruelingly repetitive and little fun—yet the system worked. With first draft in hand, and following a night's rest,

I'd read the piece through carefully, concentrating only on spelling (this was before computer spell-checkers). A second read focused on punctuation, and so on seemingly forever, reading again and again—for accuracy, clarity, tightness, tone (which must be tailored to topic and audience), vocabulary (again, appropriate to your envisioned reader), clichés (either eliminate or twist them into fresh new shapes), transitions, euphemisms (those irksome enemies of truth and precision), inappropriate jargon (inappropriate, that is, to topic or audience), "cutisms" (given my fondness for puns, alliteration and other low humor, this remains an ongoing personal battle), figurative language (too much, too little, too purple, too plain?), effectiveness of lead and closing and so on ad-bloody-nauseam. On a clunky old IBM Selectric, no less.

Such a regimen is—well, a regimen. But it not only works, it's a great way to internalize all the compositional elements just named and more, so that as time goes along you find your drafts getting cleaner and tighter faster, with less *conscious* attention to individual small battles. Take it or leave it as you wish, along with the following specific revision suggestions.

Change your perspective: Most writers these days write and revise on computers. But to write and revise *only* on-screen is to blindside yourself. If you've ever had a piece published, or seen galley or page proofs (pages edited, typographically designed and set into type, then returned for the author's inspection and approval before publication), you know how different a piece looks in print than it did on-screen. Problems that were invisible on the monitor glare like stoplights from the published page. The good news is that you can gain similar visual and critical distance throughout the revision process by occasionally printing your manuscript, double-spaced, and editing pen-on-paper, the good old-fashioned way. I revise each manuscript several times on screen, until it feels absolutely finished, then print and revise on paper—

which revisions often are shockingly heavy, given the piece's previous "done" status—enter those changes in the computer; edit again on-screen; print again, and so on until it's as clean as it can be.

Keep progressive computer files: I learned this from one of America's most successful freelance writers, Tim Cahill. Each time Tim sits down to revise a magazine piece (or book chapter), he copies the file so that the previous edit remains intact. Thus, he winds up with a growing chain of related files— "Sharks," "Sharks2," "Sharks3"—and on. This way you can toss out entire passages as you work, knowing they'll be back there, somewhere, in one file version or another, should you ever want to resurrect them. Aldo Leopold advised that the first rule of intelligent tinkering is to save all the pieces. He was referring to nature, but it's just as true for nature writing.

Talk to yourself: Toward the end of the revision process, read the piece aloud, to yourself, as if you were reading in public. This drill helps point out contractions that do or don't work, clumsy wording, awkward punctuation, tricky or ostentatious vocabulary, cutisms and other flaws. When I'm working with an editor who knows enough about creativity to let me get away with it, I even go so far as to punctuate by ear, placing my commas and such not necessarily where the grammar books demand, but where natural pauses occur in reading—the longer the pause, the stronger the punctuation.

Give it a rest: When you've revised and revised and gotten a piece as good as you can get it, put it down and walk away— take a hike in the woods and try not to think about writing, or much of anything else: "mobile meditation," I call it. Which isn't so hard, since by this terminal stage in the writing process you'll likely be sick of the sucker anyhow. Walk away and stay away for as long as you can manage.

But in order to earn this luxury of cooling-off time, as a professional at least, you must juggle several writing projects at once. As Thomas Aquinas Daly says of his painting routine: "I never work on a single piece at a time. Working on several paintings alternately, in little bites of time, I feel that I maintain a fresh outlook and a degree of objectivity that I lose when I drone away incessantly on one image." Keep two or more writing projects always in the works, at various stages, and you'll never get bored or legitimately "blocked." I find a two-week break between the "final" edit and the "final-final" edit to be about right, when deadlines (and financial desperation) allow. When you do return to the piece after a time away, you'll find that you've magically gained critical distance; the writing, whether it strikes you as awful or awesome, now will seem surprisingly unfamiliar, almost as if it had been written by someone else—allowing you yet *another* go at profitable revision.

Don't overdo it: Amidst all this advice to revise and revise and revise, there lurks the danger of revising a piece to death: "Overwriting" is the term. Another danger is using endless revision to delay submitting your efforts to the acid test of the marketplace then moving along to something new—even as redundant research can become an excuse to never start writing. But such dodges are problems primarily for dilettantes and dabblers; when you write for a living, or for any serious reason, you either keep swimming hard forward, or you sink and suffocate. Your goal is to find a personal pace of revision, and a routine to enforce it, which you can comfortably maintain over the long-haul.

Revision is fun. Well, at least it doesn't have to be boring. Not if you're doing it right. In fact, it's my favorite part of the writing process, as it is for many another. For one thing, it's easier than research and blank-page composition; a lot easier. For another, revision is the cradle of creativity. Ann Zwinger, the well-loved Colorado nature writer and artist, says it well when she calls revision "the elegance of writing. ... That's when you play, dance, sing with words, sometimes even gallop to the wind. The editing process—the refining, the thinking, the letting your mind play with connections, cutting—is the exhilarating part of writing. It's as if you're making a beautiful stock and you've put all the good things in it, and you take it off the stove and it tastes fair. But if you boil it down to a third, it gains in intensity, it gains in flavor, it gains something ineffable."

In my experience, that "ineffable" something to be gained through careful, caring revision is—professionalism.

Optional exercise

In your next writing project, incorporate each of the above suggestions into the revision stage, to determine what works for you and what doesn't. And if you're not presently a dedicated rewriter, promise yourself to revise your next essay at least ten times—hardly excessive by professional standards—beginning with a complete first draft. See what comes of it.

Erasing the Blue-pencil Blues

How to Keep Editors from "Butchering" Your Work

IF YOU'RE A PUBLISHED WRITER who's ever felt that too many of the essays and/or books you've worked so diligently to create wind up getting edited too harshly, then I don't need to tell you about the "blue-pencil blues"; you know the ailment all too well, even if the term is new. Yet, while I'd never say you should consider being heavily edited a blessing, I will suggest, ironically, that your writing can benefit greatly from it. At least it can if you have the proper professional outlook. As T. S. Eliot is said to have mused: "Some editors are failed writers, but so are most writers."

During the dozen years I spent as a moonlight freelancer and full-time staff editor—gaining thus a good view of the relative greenness of the grass on both sides of the writer/editor fence— I noted six consistent compositional problems, in my own writing as well as the work of others, that invariably prompt editors to edit. By learning to recognize and weed out these persistent troublemakers before submitting your work to a publisher, you can significantly reduce the need for editing and—a lucrative spin-off—increase sales. In order to erase the blue-pencil blues, aim for the following villains and shoot to kill.

1. Sloppy mechanics: If an editor is sufficiently impressed with the content of an essay or book, she may invest significant labor in editing for grammar, punctuation, spelling and all the other hardware that holds a manuscript together—

though she'd really rather not and rightly so, since basic, college-level manuscript mechanics are the writer's responsibility. But most often, most editors have neither the time nor the inclination to wallow in such sophomoric basics. Consequently, sloppily prepared manuscripts peppered with mechanical glitches that could easily have been caught and corrected by the writer, and should have been, are rarely going to sell. And the few that do are sure to be heavily edited.

The self-evident remedy here is to make sure your copy is so tight it squeaks when read. If *you* don't see to the mechanical essentials and your editors have to, consider their tinkering a blessing, not butchery, and keep your complaints to yourself. Once again: Keep in close touch with Strunk & White.

2. Out-of-style: In the world of books, "voice" is largely the writer's choice. But among magazines, each has its own coveted style and expects its writers to comply, within reason if not to the letter. A serious freelancer knows this and—while making no attempt to parrot a publication's every stylistic inflection—will avoid submitting seriously off-key pieces. You wouldn't, for example, use a stiff, academic voice in an essay bound for a magazine whose style is informal, conversational and lightly humorous—or would you? While many attempt it, few succeed.

And vice-versa, of which I can offer a recently humbling personal example. This past winter I was invited to participate in a fund-raising reading for a local nonprofit children's nature-study group. I've done a lot of readings, for big crowds and small, and it's generally a breeze. But this was different in that the large local audience would be peppered with neighbors and friends. Of even greater concern was that I'd be reading with Terry Tempest Williams; not someone I'd wish to embarrass with a poor team showing. Consequently, as the time drew near I became somewhat obsessed, laboriously creating an original piece of personal narrative tailored to my (fairly informed) perception of the audience's expectations, rewriting and rehearsing until I had it all but memorized. Going for a bit of humor—always a good bet for public readings, which can be boring and stodgy—I got heavily into word-play and delivered the reading (zonked on adrenaline) with dramatic vigor.

To my great surprise and greater relief, it was a smashing success. For months the compliments rolled in, until, gradually, I became persuaded that here, perhaps, was something a cut above my average creation—something fit, perhaps, for publication in a major East Coast magazine, which elite and insular market I'd rarely approached. So I asked my agent to send it around. Honoring my request without comment, Carl sent the piece, titled "Logging On" (a double entendre, referring to the irony that I earn my living on a computer while heating my home with wood) to *The Atlantic Monthly*—which promptly and justifiably rejected it as "overwritten."

Thus jolted, I suddenly recognized that "Logging On" *was* overwritten—for print. Had I not been slightly sloshed on praise I'd have realized that what succeeds when read with vocal enthusiasm to a live and lively audience of a couple-hundred fellow nature nuts—specifically my made-for-the-stage word play—might be all too much for such as *The Atlantic Monthly*.

A submission that's written in a voice that's gratingly off-key to a publication's style, such as mine to *The Atlantic Monthly*, tells an editor that the writer either hasn't bothered to familiarize himself with the magazine (admittedly, being rural and western, I'm not an avid *TAM* reader), or is unable to recognize a distinct house style when he sees it. Most such wildshots will be eagerly rejected, as was mine, even if submitted by an agent. And the few that are accepted will either be returned for massive revision, or necessarily "butchered" by an editor.

Moral: Know each of your markets personally, and pitch your voice accordingly.

(Postscript: With too much time, work and ego invested in "Logging On" to just let it die, I revised the piece several times more, toning down the stagey stuff, and submitted it to the most artful and literary of "green" magazines, *Orion*. To my extreme delight they accepted it—then set about further improving the piece by pointing out several subtle non sequiturs I had overlooked. We're never too old, or too experienced, not to gain from loss—so long as we can see and accept the reality of our ongoing fallibility).

3. Length: When I queried one of my favorite magazines with an article idea recently, the editor gave me a go, but stipulated that the length not exceed fifteen-hundred words; brutally brief by my wordy standards. Yet, had I sent him the twenty-five hundred words I generated on first draft, I could hardly have taken rational umbrage had he chainsawed the honker down to the requested length—or, more likely, kicked it back as beyond the bounds of our agreement.

Having learned this lesson in the long-ago, it's a rule I try never to break. In my years as an editor, I rejected scores of otherwise publishable manuscripts simply because they were so far beyond the specified length and I cared neither to hack them down myself nor to cajole or bully the writers into doing it. Compared to compromise, rejection is easy.

Moral: When an editor or writer's guidelines "suggest" maximum and/or minimum lengths, listen—or lose.

4. Accuracy: Consider this scenario: You've written and submitted an article in which you quote, from a telephone interview, a source named Peterson. The piece sells, is published and all is well—until the day your editor sends you a copy of a letter received from Mr. Petersen, who's miffed that you spelled his name wrong. Likewise and justifiably, your editor is pissed because he feels compelled to print Petersen's cranky letter of complaint along with a public apology. How eager do you think either of them will be to work with you again?

In addition to bungled names, common manuscript inaccuracies include dates, figures, the wording and attribution of quotes, titles and place-names. Take the time, make the effort, to verify.

5. Completeness and accessibility: Never assume your readers will have sufficient foreknowledge of your topic to fill in significant informational blanks for themselves. When in doubt—particularly in explication and argumentation—err on the side of too much background detail; those who already know it all will rarely resent a brief review, which serves merely to confirm their wisdom.

6. Clarity: Clarity is the foundation of effective communication—and effective communication is the cornerstone of good writing. To achieve clarity, polish every manuscript until it sparkles. Next, ask a qualified friend or family member—any literate person who's willing to assume the risky role of candid critic—to read the bit and point out any haze or fog. If your reader is confused by a word or a passage or grimaces at an awkward metaphor or joke or otherwise misses a point you've thought you've made, it's a fair bet that others, including editors, will hit similar walls.

Certainly, a good editor can polish your muddy prose—that's part of what she's paid to do. But a serious writer won't expect her to, won't want her to, won't give her the chance.

Of course, all this talk of how to minimize having your work "butchered" assumes you'll be dealing with competent editors; a fair assumption, for the most part. Slovenly and unqualified editors are scarce as fur on a fish and ephemeral as teenage love. In general, you can trust career blue-pencilers to be skilled professionals dedicated to making their publications look good by making their writers look, and perform, their best. As Dan Crockett, one of my favorite magazine honchos (*Bugle*), describes the ideal literary relationship, the writer and editor work not at odds but as partners, "as if building a mortarless stone wall, trading turns fitting the next rock."

That's how it should be, and, in my experience, that's how it mostly is. When an editor improves my words without making them sound more like his than mine, I'm unabashedly grateful. But as much as I appreciate the help, I always do my best to leave no loose ends to tighten, no fat to trim, no murky prose to clarify, no errors to correct or blanks to fill in, and no off-key voice to grate against house style. That's my challenge and duty as a writer. While I don't always succeed, I do always try. Likewise, when I'm sitting on the editor's side of the desk, I try to make every essay or book I work on as good as it can be *without destroying the writer's voice*. That's my challenge and duty as an editor.

Certainly and sadly, I do occasionally encounter an utterly incompetent editor. But these unqualified few are blessedly mobile, either learning fast or shifting to employment more suitable to their talents, such as censoring mail at a prison or editing real estate listings. In the majority of instances, if my prose, or yours, gets heavily edited, it's our fault, not the editor's.

Thus, the most consistently reliable way to avoid the feeling that your work is being "butchered" by others is to bear down harder with your own sharp knife.

CHAPTER 14

Selling Your Soul

This Little Piggie Went to Market ...

*Dear Contributor: Thank you for not sending us anything lately.
It suits our present needs.* —from *Peanuts*, by Charles Schulz

NATURE WRITING SHOULD be motivated by the love of nature and the writing process, with or without hope of publication. Still, writing without publishing is like chewing without swallowing, smoking without inhaling or love without sex—you can *do* it, you can even enjoy it, yet you'll always be left feeling somehow ... incomplete.

The hard truth is that getting published *well* (as opposed, say, to the letters column in your local fish-wrapper), especially the first few times, has never been a breeze and is getting no easier fast. Nor can I offer much help in the commercial realm; this book is not a marketing guide, but only what its title suggests: a somewhat eccentric but absolutely earnest guide to experiencing, loving, thinking and writing honestly and well about nature—wild nature, human nature, *your* nature—in ways that may (we both must hope) prove at least personally meaningful. Beyond that, what you do with what you write sloshes beyond this particular pale.

Except to say that if you're good, I'd love to read you in a good magazine or book someday. In fact, a significant part of my motivation for taking on this challenging book is to encourage the sort of perception and writing that might help open new eyes to the beauty, joy and *necessity* of personally experiencing and working to preserve what's left of truly wild nature; what's left of beauty and sanity in this human world gone virtually mad.

"A world of *made*," warns lower-case poet e. e. cummings, "is not a world of *born*."

Culture is made.

Nature is born.

Certainly, the only way your writing can ever hope to positively influence either or both of those worlds is to find its way into print. Still and again, this book is not that book. That book (foremost among others) is *Writer's Market*, a massive, annually updated compilation of "8,000 editors who buy what you write." Continuing with the overtly commercial cover come-ons, from the 1999 edition:

Now Includes Agents!
989 new publishing opportunities
1,534 consumer magazines
464 trade magazines
1,170 book publishers
250 script buyers
6,500 phone & fax numbers
4,000 e-mail addresses & websites
1,120 pages
Specific editorial needs & submission guidelines
Pay Rates, Royalties and Advances

Additionally, every edition of *Writer's Market* revisits all the marketing essentials. A section titled "Getting Published: Articles and information for previously unpublished writers," includes primers on developing ideas and targeting markets, writing book proposals, query and cover letters, finding and working with agents, professional courtesy, tools of the trade, manuscript format, submitting photographs, tracking your submissions and more—deadly boring stuff for the most part, but absolutely essential as well. Also in the "Getting Published" section you'll find a "Query Letter Clinic," tips for using the Internet for research and more.

A second front-matter *WM* feature, "Personal Views," offers a selection of "inspirational" pieces from such overnight stars as Sebastian Junger (*The Perfect Storm*), all implying "If I can do it, so can you!" (Well ...)

A third, more matter-of-fact feature, "The Business of Writing: Information for the more experienced writer," includes discussions of contract negotiation, payment rates, online markets and an overview of the book-publishing world.

Completing this helpful prefatory section of the big book is a bit on agents, including a general discussion of that mysterious profession, complete with a listing of agents who welcome hearing from newcomers. (Not all do; more in a moment.)

Skipping to the back-matter, *WM* offers informed and intriguing overviews of scriptwriting, writer's syndicates, greeting card markets, contests and awards, plus general and book publisher's indexes.

But the meat of this helpful monster is the fifty categories of markets, broken into such general groupings as, for example (focusing on our specific concerns): "Animals," "Nature, Conservation & Ecology" and "Sports," the latter including such nature-based outdoor recreations as hunting and fishing, hiking and backpacking and a whole bunch more. To demonstrate how the listings work, the most useful approach is simply to quote a representative verbatim sample:

AMC Outdoors: The Magazine of the Appalachian Mountain Club. Appalachian Mountain Club, 5 Joy St., Boston MA 02108. (617) 523-0655 ext. 312. Fax: (617) 523-0722. E-mail: amcoutdoors@ mcimail.com.

Contact: Editor/publisher. 90% freelance written. Monthly magazine covering outdoor recreation and conservation issues in the Northeast. Estab. 1907. Circ. 66,000. Pays on publication. Publishes ms. an average of 3 months after acceptance. Byline given. Offers 25% kill fee. Buys all rights. Editorial lead time 3 months. Submit seasonal material 4 months in advance. Reports in 1 month on queries; 2 months on mss. Sample copy for 9x12 SASE. Writer's guidelines free.

Nonfiction: Book excerpts, essays, exposé, general interest, historical/nostalgic, how-to, interview/profile, opinion, personal experience, photo feature, technical, travel. Special issues: Northern Forest Report (April) featuring the northern areas of New York, New Hampshire, Vermont, and Maine, and protection efforts for these areas. Buys 10 mss/year. Query with or without published clips. Length: 500–3,000 words. Sometimes pays expenses of writers on assignment.

Photos: State availability of photos with submission. Reviews contact sheets, transparencies and prints. Model releases and identification of subjects required.

Columns/Departments: News (environmental/outdoor recreation coverage of Northeast), 1,300 words. Buys 20 mss/year. Query. Pays $50–500."

Discussion: This listing, like most in *WM*, provides much of what you need to know to decide whether or not this magazine is a potential market for your style and topics, how big and otherwise "good" a market it is, how to go about submitting a query or manuscript and to whom. Specifically: "Byline given" is good news (incredibly, some pubs do not), as is the industry-standard 25 percent kill fee, payable should you and the magazine contract for a piece of work that you deliver on schedule and in publishable form, but the editor decides not to use.

Payment on publication, however, stinks, ameliorated somewhat in this instance by a relatively short lead time of three to four months (it's not unusual to have "accepted" articles get shelved for a year or more before seeing print), reducing the time you have to sit and stew between delivering your work and getting paid. Still, unless your ego or your dog is starving, the standard professional advice is to avoid doing business with pay-on-publication periodicals, since such a writer-unfriendly system suggests either greed on the part of the publisher or weak finances or both, assuring you lots of frustration and little else—granting one important class of exceptions, to wit:

Many nature and environmental magazines, including some of the otherwise best outlets for nature writing, are published on bootlace budgets by nonprofit organizations. Even here there are limits—after all, the editors and other employees of these magazines take home regular paychecks, so why shouldn't freelance contributors? Yet, if paying on publication helps a good rag to squeak by, I may go along with it. And too—taking it down to the wire—in the genre of pure nature writing, good periodical outlets are so precious few, and competition from other writers so staggering, that sometimes, either you play by the publishers' rules or go stand in the corner by yourself.

While full-time freelancers can hardly avoid buying a copy of *Writer's Market* every other year or so, it's probably not worth its price for occasional use ($27.99 for the 1999 number, in paperback). Every public library this side of Wolf Hole, Arizona, keeps a current copy of *WM* in the reference section; go have a look before you leap.

Urgent tip: In addition to reading the *Writer's Market* listings, always, *always* study *at least* the most recent issue of any magazine you intend to hit with an article query or manuscript *before* you submit. Study for what? For content, editorial style and politics, general character of audience (often revealed by the products and services being advertised) and for recent publication of articles by other writers on topics that too-closely parallel your own. A would-be contributor's lack of familiarity with a magazine is often obvious to editors, being the equivalent of a face-slapping insult and assuring the death of the sale, if not the salesman. Take the time to familiarize yourself with each potential market in advance, or risk experiencing the truth of Oliver Herford's definition of a manuscript as "something submitted in haste and returned at leisure."

(Postscript: After reading the above in manuscript, I received the following cautionary addendum from *Orion* editor H. Emerson Blake: "I'm glad you emphasized that while useful as a starting point, *Writer's Market* should not be a shortcut; writers should do real, substantial research into all the publications for which their writing might work. There are many magazines not listed in *WM*—including some small, regional publications that are just the place new writers should be trying to get their first foothold. I encourage writers in my workshops to create a chart of all the magazines to which they might send their work and post it on their office walls. *Orion* is not in *WM*—I withdrew the listing because it overwhelmed me with submissions, eighty or ninety percent of which were off the mark. I could almost always tell the submissions that were generated from *WM* by their content.")

For book authors, a second marketing reference worth introducing here is Michael Larsen's *How to Write a Book Proposal*. Within the limited scope of its title, this one has it all—to the point that anyone (including my one and only dearest daughter) who asks me for advice on writing book proposals gets the pat answer: "Read *How to Write a Book Proposal*." Here again, most competent libraries have a copy. In lieu of a review, I'll simply refer you to the back-cover promo, which tells it like it is (inappropriate exclamations and other typically overblown PR prose notwithstanding), like so:

You may have the hottest book idea of the year, but you'll need a well-crafted proposal to get an agent's or editor's attention, a book contract, and a healthy advance on royalties!

Written by a literary agent who has successfully placed authors' manuscripts with more than sixty publishers, this book takes you through every step of writing a nonfiction book proposal, showing you exactly how to:

- test the market potential of your idea and effectively communicate that potential in your proposal
- prepare a succinct introduction that distills the essence of your idea, reveals your book's scope and audience, and compels an editor to read on
- pick the best editors and publishers to pitch your proposal to
- create a professional-looking proposal package
- predispose a publisher to make you their best offer.

You'll also find a complete sample proposal to use as a guide, a list of surefire outline verbs that will add punch to any proposal, a nine-point Idea Test to check the salability of your book ideas, and a wealth of inside tips on winning the proposal-writing game. Even if your book is already completed or self-published, you'll learn why you should prepare a proposal anyway and how it can be your most effective selling tool.

You supply the ideas—this book will show you how to put together a proposal package that will help you get the best possible editor, publisher, and deal for your book!

And that it truly will, to the extent *any* how-to manual can work such miracles.

Shifting gears a cog or two, here's a word of caution regarding book publishers: Beware of subsidy, or "vanity" presses—those ego-leeches who lure overly eager would-be authors into paying all production, promotion and distribution costs and a big fat fee to boot. If you have a book worth publishing, there's a *real* house out there, somewhere, willing to risk *its* funds on the venture. If you believe in yourself and your book, *keep searching*; there are hundreds of possibilities to probe.

Now, at last and at least, a few words about, and from, literary agents. First, about: "Changing literary agents is like changing deck chairs on the *Titanic*." (Can't recall who said it first.) Which is by way of asking you to ask yourself: Do you really *need* an agent? Many successful writers take it upon themselves to learn the marketing ropes and do just fine, thank you, on their own. The widespread belief among aspiring writers that "If only I had an agent, I'd be getting published" is largely bogus.

And then there's the Catch-22 aphorism that says "You can't get an agent unless you've already published a book," which, most often, is true. As it happened, I sold my first three books on my own, without an agent, to small publishing houses— and through those three experiences, I got "royally screwed" only once. (Which was once more than enough.) Even so and even today, I market my nonfiction children's books on my own (a sideline that helps subsidize my nature writing), since I know those ropes well and trust my long-time publisher.

And keep in mind also that an agent's fees will soak up 15 or 20 percent of your book advances and royalties. Additionally, some agents (none I'd work with) demand that you reimburse them for such standard business expenses as phone calls, photocopies, etc., incurred (ostensibly) in the course of trying to market your manuscripts, win or lose.

Yet, for the past several years, I have had an agent. A fine agent. An agent I'd not want to be without. In addition to steering me toward viable book projects and away from potential disasters, my agent earns his fee through contract interpretation and bargaining alone, negotiating better deals than I could ever manage myself. And most important of all, he's an honest and supportive critic, a trusted friend and advisor—which is a whole lot more than many agents offer.

Preferring always to get my water directly from the spring, I asked one of New York's most experienced and respected literary agents, Carl D. Brandt, what general advice he would offer to writers shopping for competent representation, and specifically for his views on agents who charge a "reading fee" to review book proposals. Here is Carl's response:

> I believe the best way to approach an agent is with a good letter. Most agents are interested in long-term relationships, and consequently want to know something about potential clients, how they see themselves, what kind of writing they want to do and why, how they envision the directions they hope to take in the future, and their experience writing (in whatever form), as well as their experience with the world. Then, of course, the writer should mention the particular project at hand, but relatively briefly. If the agent is interested in the writer and the project, he or she will ask to see an outline and chapters.
>
> There is an association of agents called, appropriately, the Association of Authors' Representatives, and we are bound to a strict Canon of Ethics. Amongst those canons is one prohibiting reading fees. There is something very logical and pleasingly simple about the notion that if the author eats, the agent eats (and the reverse).
>
> There are obvious things that an author can expect from an agent—financial probity first and foremost. An agent can't always sell salable work, let alone unsalable work; but the point, I think, is that the agent should be trying with what's at hand, while at the same time keeping an eye out for the long view.

Agents are a bit like writers in the sense that all they have to invest is their time. Most of us feel, rightly or wrongly, that we're already overcommitted; consequently, when an agent responds to a writer's query by saying he or she is too busy to take on new clients right then, odds are good that's the precise truth. Consequently, such a "rejection" letter should not be taken personally, and it should not be regarded as a comment on the worth of the work or indeed the worth of the writer.

Moreover, I'm confident Mr. Brandt would second my clichéd-but-true suggestion to the effect that "If at first you don't succeed, try and try again—elsewhere."

Gail Hochman, Carl's partner in Brandt & Hochman, Literary Agents, Inc., likewise suggests that writers approach agents with a letter of self-introduction:

Usually an agent can tell from a good query letter whether the subject of the book and the publishing or professional credits of the author might be a potential match for that agent. Since we're all pretty overloaded with reading, screening query letters allows us to ask to receive and read material that might actually fall within our area of interest and expertise.

It's not too hard for a writer to assemble a list of good potential agents. Presumably a writer seeking publication is also a reader, and will have developed a sense of which books out there are similar in tone, sensibility, genre, etc., to his own manuscripts. The acknowledgments page of these books will often mention the agent. Or a call to the subsidiary rights department of a publisher should yield the name of a book's agent. (When asked about the availability of film rights or of the author for a public speaking event, a caller will usually be referred to the book's agent.) Or try the Author's Guild Registry. This small amount of legwork by a potential client will be impressive to a potential agent, *and* it will save the writer from wasting time pursuing really unlikely matches.

Finally, there is no dearth of books and publications that help authors learn more about particular agents and editors. A search of *Publisher's Weekly, Writer's Digest, Poets & Writers* et al. will yield terrific information about agents. Again, most of us are impressed (or even flattered) that a writer bothered to do some research and came up with our name. I prefer to deal with responsible clients who are willing to do a bit of intelligent research regarding where they might fit into the publishing scene, rather than someone whose query letter boasts mainly that this manuscript will be my next bestseller.

And that's the New York truth.

Don't Give Up Your Day Job

(At least not prematurely)

AN OLD BLUEGRASS SONG, repeating an old folk saying, candidly warns aspiring professional musicians: "Don't give up your day job." That is: Just because you've landed a few bar-band gigs and your mother thinks you're wonderful doesn't necessarily mean you can convert your part-time passion into a full-time profession. It might. But most likely it doesn't. Making it as a professional musician is a rocky old row to hoe. It's highly competitive and whimsical, and a brutal buyer's market.

Same-same with writing.

If you hanker to write full-time, great. But *work* your way into it rather than diving in blindly, backed only by optimism. Trouble is, even if you can earn enough, month after month after year, to survive in this increasingly feudalistic Global Economy (and few full-time freelancers can), you'll rarely know *when* those checks you've so well earned will appear in your mailbox. Budgeting will be difficult at best. Your mornings will hang in desperate anticipation, awaiting the mail. Disappointment will plague your afternoons as doubt will haunt your dreams.

I know, having lived it for decades.

Once upon a time, and for a good long while, I had a dandy day job as western editor for *Mother Earth News* (the funky old good version), commuting via computer from the little cabin my wife calls the Dog House, high on a Colorado mountainside, to the home offices in North Carolina. Then the magazine was sold into unwise hands and not long after into

bankruptcy. (It's now back in print, under different owner-
ship.) Most of my former fellow staff writers and editors soon
found good new jobs. But because I was, and remain, unwilling to trade the bugling of Rocky Mountain elk—which, on
quiet September nights, Caroline and I can hear from bed—
for screaming city sirens, I was prompted by desperation to
risk the leap to full-time freelancing, which previously had
been only a vigorous moonlight venture backed by *MEN* (and
before that, by part-time teaching).

Since then—a dozen acutely interesting years it has been—
I've survived on less gross income per month, on average,
than many "middle-class" Americans lay out in SUV pay-
ments alone. But how much I earn freelancing, or fail to earn,
isn't always the worst of it. I know of few other professions so
burdened with low *and* slow pay as independent writing,
especially in the nature/natural history/green genre.

It's natural to blame slow payment on the editors for whom
we work. And certainly, they can at times be the problem—
like one of my (otherwise) favorites, who repeatedly forgets,
for weeks and even months at a stretch, to submit payment
vouchers to accounting for articles contracted, delivered and
(most often silently) accepted; even knowing, as he does, the
grief it causes me; even as he draws a regular paycheck every
two weeks. To euphemize a popular scatological cliché, "Poop
happens." (I now give magazines a month or so to pay, depending on their past performance and how strapped I am, before
becoming a persistent pest.)

Even so and happily, most editors, most of the time, would
rather see their writers smiling than angry, and give their care
and feeding an appropriately high priority, priding themselves when prompt payment can be made. I use the inactive
voice here—"can be made"—because most often it's not editors, but greedy (or merely penny-pinching) publishers and/or
anal-retentive bean-counters who hold things up, making life

difficult for freelance contributors as well as the editors who have to absorb their ire. Consider these responses from 189 consumer and trade magazine editors when asked by *Publishing News* some years ago about the average time elapsed between submitting payment requests for freelance contributions, and the mailing of those checks:

> Within 10 days 32.8%
> 11–29 days 39.2%
> 30–60 days 24.3%
> Longer 1.1%
> Don't know 1.1%
> No response 1.5%

What bothers me most, from a professional point of view, is the collective 2.6 percent of editors in the last two categories who could just as well have responded: "Don't give a damn."

More heartening is that roughly one-third of the magazines surveyed attempted to mail checks within ten days of the time an editor issued a check request; I only wish I wrote for more of them, and that more editors cut those critical check requests faster. Most of the magazines I regularly work for fall within the 64.6 percent who take two (not bad) to eight (very bad) weeks, *or longer*, to pay.

And all of the magazines in this survey, remember, were so-called pay-on-*acceptance* pubs. Pay-on-publication periodicals, no matter their sublime goals in life, are usually either under-financed or published by people—or, more often, corporations—with the moral integrity of the so-called "wise use" so-called "movement." Consequently, on-pub payment is not only excruciatingly slow, but generally low as well. In my ingenuous youth, I once waited nearly two years between the time I submitted an article *on assignment* and had it accepted, to when it was finally published and my pitiful pittance arrived. That experience was a low-end epiphany in my freelancing career. These days, I would rather (and sometimes do) eat peanut butter sandwiches for a month than give in to the pay-on-pub sluggards. (Not-for-profit, nature-friendly exceptions previously and once again noted, when I can afford it.)

In my battle-scarred opinion, only fools and beginners—of which I have been both—do otherwise. If *every last stinking writer* would unite to boycott payment on publication, that usurious old villain would quickly bite the dust. But alas, in a profession embodying so much *ego hunger*, especially among new writers craving publication and financially secure part-timers to whom income is not a major issue, that will never be.

Certainly, book-writing is potentially more lucrative and secure than magazine freelancing. Most book publishers, even the small ones, pay more on advance than most magazines pay most writers for most articles. And if the book sells well enough to earn back its advance, it may pay semi-annual royalties for years. Get a good gig going writing cookbooks, diet books, New Age self-help hokum, celebrity biographies or sappy sonatas on "Why I Love My Doggies," and you've got it made.

If that's how you want to invest your creative energies.

But that's not nature writing, which, so sadly, isn't a mass-market commodity in this increasingly de-natured and virtual world of made. Even the most wildly celebrated nature writers rarely earn enough from writing alone to sustain even a modestly comfortable "middle-class" lifestyle, much less to afford such "luxuries" as health insurance. Rather, most must supplement their writing income with frequent travel—teaching workshops, giving readings, speeches and the like. I for one would rather sit at home and "type" (as Caroline calls it), rewarded each evening by a long, slow, leaf-drop-quiet walk in the woods.

While I could live without writing, I could never live without the things I write about.

To each …

All of this, and more unsaid, is why I earnestly counsel against plunging prematurely into full-time nature writing unless you have a bank account large enough to carry you through those long and unpredictable voids between paychecks, and don't mind seeing your savings consumed in the process. I have none such today and never have had. But neither do I have a choice, my dice—personal as well as financial—having long ago been irretrievably cast. In redundant summation, I advise you not to give up your day job for full-time nature writing until and unless you've put away shekels enough to see you through. Otherwise, you're guaranteed to suffer. Particularly so in the start-up phase, which typically lasts for years. Just how large a nest-egg you need depends on your lifestyle, your bottom-line monthly overhead and an *honest* evaluation of your immediate and long-term earning ability as a writer.

And how to amass that cushion of cash? By writing, of course. Writing and saving and patience. With every slow paycheck you deposit in your "creative freedom account," you'll also be accruing professional skills, experience and contacts.

It's hard, but it's true.

CHAPTER 15

Talking the Walk

Rating Writers' Workshops

*In order to write a book, it is necessary to sit down (or stand up)
and write. Therein lies the difficulty.* —Edward Abbey

OLD FRIEND ABBEY didn't think much of writers' workshops,
and neither do a lot of other established professionals who've
moved beyond what workshops have to offer. In his *Field
Guide to Writing Fiction*, A. B. Guthrie, Jr., near the end of his
writing career and life, had this to say about workshopping:

> The trouble with writers' colonies as I know them is talk. Here
> the brethren come, full of themselves, each full of enthusi-
> asm for the work he is going to write and can't wait to get
> around to. He can't wait, either, to explain his great idea to
> his fellows. So he tells them and tells them, waiting with
> some impatience while they take their ebullient turns. He
> goes on day by day, telling his story idea over and over again
> until it stales in his mind. Each telling has diminished his
> inner impetus, has worn away at his first fine urge to put
> words on paper. "Well," he says to himself then, "I guess my
> idea wasn't too good in the first place. I'll get a new inspira-
> tion, soon." And never, in all that time, has he written a fresh
> word. Coroner's verdict: Death by gabble. The professional
> writer talks little about his project or projects. He may name
> the general subject, report how he's getting along, and that's
> it. He saves his words for paper.

Elsewhere, still in an uncharacteristically grumpy mood, Guthrie adds: "His story finished (he thinks), the tyro is likely to show it around, to friends, kinsmen, and other beginners, asking for their honest opinions though what he wishes for is praise."

Had my old friend forgotten that in his own writing youth—he'd been a newspaper journalist for more than twenty years, but didn't start writing seriously (*The Big Sky*) until age forty-five—Bud attended the first-ever Breadloaf Writer's Conference, under the direction of some frosty old fellow who liked to wax poetically about such nonsense as "the road less traveled"?

Finally along this negative line, in *The Green Hills of Africa*, Hemingway muses that "Writers should work alone. They should see each other only after their work is done, and not too often then." Yet, at least as self-documented in *A Moveable Feast*, the young, hungry Ernie thrived on the company and conversation of his seniors and peers.

What gives?

All the above naysaying notwithstanding, the most personally informed, objective and humane explication of the value of writers' workshops I've yet encountered comes from H. Emerson Blake, managing editor of *Orion*, the prestigious quarterly magazine "of people and nature." As Chip testifies:

> I've taught a few writing workshops, and there are problems. However, there are always some participants who are after something other than just getting published—after some kind of understanding of the world they've previously been denied or didn't know about. These folks come to the workshops, and to their journal-keeping and writing, without any intention of getting published, but just to get to know themselves and their longings better. I have a lot of respect for these people and find great satisfaction in corroborating their experience ...

people just out of marriages, people in career transition, once a woman whose son had recently been killed, another whose husband had tragically died in an auto accident, older people winding down their lives, all of them having returned to nature to help make sense of life. They're about half the people; the gratifying half that make it all worthwhile. The other half ask questions like "How wide should the margins on the manuscript be?"

Read carefully enough and editor Blake has just described the difference between good workshopping and bad: the mindsets of the participants themselves. Absolutely, the quality of the "facilitators" bears on the value of a workshop, but only secondarily to "student" expectations, preparation and participation.

Being a loner socially as well as professionally, and always broke to boot, I've never attended a writers' colony or workshop as a student, or belonged to any writers' group. I have, however, talked to writers' groups and participated in writing workshops as an instructor, resulting in experiences and impressions more closely confirming those of Chip Blake than those of Bud Guthrie.

Most recently and memorably, I taught a four-day naturewriting seminar at the Yellowstone Institute—a rustic, no-frills natural history and arts retreat run by the Yellowstone Association and housed in the wildest road-accessible corner of the world's first national park. Class size was limited to fourteen, an eclectic lot ranging from a young woman Yellowstone Park ranger who wanted to interpret nature in children's books, to a retired octogenarian Roman Catholic priest with an intriguing (borderline heretical) interest in "nature mysticism." One grandmother had recently lost two family members and, her doctrinal religion (apparently) having failed her, was searching, via writing and nature, for a reason to go on. Not a blessed one was of the "How wide should the margins be?" persuasion, and only one fit Guthrie's dire definition of attending a writing workshop "wishing for praise." Most were serious about their writing and had done a fair bit of it, though only a few had been published, and then mostly modestly. Laudably, most approached nature and the writing process with the humble, open-minded, inquisitive attitude of Zen practitioners.

In all, they were a joy.

And for them, save one, the most beneficial part of our time together was the last day's roundtable critique. I had asked each student to bring along a sample of his or her writing, approximately a thousand words, typed and double-spaced in proper manuscript format, with fourteen copies so that everyone in the class could read along and make notes as the writer read aloud. Saving this exercise for our final afternoon together—lounging in circular seminar-style in cool green grass beneath the flickering shade of quaking aspens a mile above the Lamar Valley road—well, it was a kick.

By encouraging the most eager and self-confident to go first, by the time it came their turn even the shiest among us felt sufficiently comfortable to offer a decent read. This, I discerned—to have an attentive audience for a "safe" group reading, and to receive honest feedback from their peers as well as from an ostensible "expert"—was a primary reason most had enrolled. After each reading, we went around the circle with every participant offering one positive comment on both the writing and the oral delivery, plus one gently constructive criticism of each. Saving my own two-bits worth for last, I often found that one or more of my "students" had beat me to my thunder; as always when teaching, I came away convinced that I'd learned far more than I'd taught.

Judging from the postpartum written evaluations, everyone was quite pleased. In fact, as previously noted, it was the strong encouragement of those generous Yellowstone writers that led me to the risky decision to go ahead with this long-delayed "guide," using my Yellowstone lecture notes as far more than an outline. I definitely got the greenest end of *that* stick.

Even so, for the most practical of reasons—time and money—I've not taught a writing workshop since Yellowstone, back in 1998. And in that decision not to teach perhaps lurks a worthwhile insight to rating writing workshops, should you ever get the urge. With the exception of some high-profile, high-price, celebrity-centered gatherings, where too often too many students enroll more to rub egos with famous writers than to learn from them, and too often those same famous writers make great celebrities but lousy instructors (any workshop led by Richard Nelson or Terry Tempest Williams or John Nichols is happily excluded from this latter disclaimer)—teaching writing workshops generally pays even less than staying home and writing.

Consequently, I for one—and I'm hardly alone—prefer to stay home and write.

Thus, as a test of quality, if a workshop leader is a gainfully employed literary professional (like, say, *Orion's* Emerson Blake), he or she is not likely there for the money, which usually isn't great, or for ego gratification, which isn't needed, but because he or she *wants* to be there, to share and to learn. However, if you've never heard of this person before, and can't track down a sample of his or her work (to judge for yourself), or at least a résumé of professional literary experience—I'd look elsewhere.

In the end, whether to workshop or not to workshop, like so much else in life, must be a personal choice. My own experience leads me to agree, somewhat, with both views: On the one hand, as Abbey proclaims, to be a writer you must sit down and *write*—"walking the talk." But writing is a lonely business and everyone needs occasional contact with peers. At the best of times that contact can be epiphanous.

While no writing workshop—no matter who sponsors or teaches it or how lovely the setting or daunting the tuition—can magically produce talent or inspiration where none exists or offer a fast limo ride to prestigious publication and public adoration, most are, if not quite alchemical, in some way and another at least instructive and often inspirational.

Moreover and perhaps best of all, if you're selective, lucky and don't take yourself too seriously, the workshop experience—like writing itself—can often be fun.

Ten Topical Tips

Something Old, Something New
(By way of a brief review and mop-up)

1. Trust yourself: My wife is my presubmissions editor, reading most everything I write and commenting candidly. And she's good at it; I take Caroline's criticisms and suggestions seriously and generally act on them. But—and here's the meat and message—not always. For example: In *Ghost Grizzlies*, while describing the tranquillity of an alpine lake at sunrise, I wrote: "Morning. A hundred yards below camp, Grizzly Lake mirrors snowy peaks. Moby trout lip the surface for bugs, leap and roll, making circular rise forms that grow concentrically outward, like well-lived lives."

When Caroline hit that fishy simile she lined it out, noting: "Doesn't make sense." Maybe not to her, and maybe not at all. Yet the image was clear to me—after all, I'd *seen* it—and, as an imagination-challenged nonfictioneer to whom literary analogy is always hard-caught, I was reluctant to toss it back. So I didn't. My editor at Henry Holt let it pass without comment, the book was released and that was that. Until the day, many months later, when I received a letter from a writer I'd never met but whose byline I recognized and respected. This generous gentleman said he liked the book, and among his favorite parts was "that great simile about trout rise-forms radiating outward 'like well-lived lives.'"

The point being (redux)—as in music, art and love—literary tastes vary wildly; what one editor, critic or reader scorns, another may well adore. Consequently, while informed criticism is invaluable and always rates serious consideration—the final vote must be yours. Vote as objectively as you can manage.

2. Keep a writer's journal: Not a "dear diary," but a logbook of potentially useful thoughts, quotations, conversations, events, titles, resources, contacts and the like. I keep just such a ledger and pilfer it shamelessly in hopes of misleading my readers and editors into thinking I have a great mind and memory.

3. Read for inspiration as well as information: This is particularly important for writers of nonfiction who (like me) attempt to excuse their ignorance of literature—fiction and poetry most especially—with the complaint that they "have to read so much for research, there's no time or energy left to read for pleasure." The best nonfiction writing (my estimation) is one-quarter information, one-quarter entertainment, one-quarter style and one-quarter philosophy. *Make* the time, *find* the energy to read widely, ranging well beyond the bounds of mere research.

4. When your writing hits the outhouse wall, go take a hike: Meditation is the best antidote to writer's block, and walking is the perfect meditation for those of us unable or unwilling to sit indoors for long periods all twisted up like human pretzels chanting baby-talk in some foreign language. Don't, however, go out walking with the conscious intent of forcing, expecting or even hoping to achieve astounding revelations. Your aim is merely a relaxing stroll in the most restful and natural setting available, your mind unchained and free to roam. I can't recall all the times this exercise (in both senses of the word) has revealed a hidden answer, found a missing link or otherwise helped breach a seemingly impenetrable creative wall. Well-behaved dogs make compatible companions; talkative humans don't.

5. Strive always for professionalism: Give a hundred percent to every writing project, no matter how large or small the magazine or book, or how much it does or doesn't pay. Always meet or beat your deadlines, make every story better than you ever thought it could be and cooperate fully in the editing process, no matter how annoying. Editors are notorious for playing musical chairs, promotion can be rapid and a junior editor at a small magazine or book press today may be a Manhattan heavy-hitter tomorrow. Strive to make every editor you deal with remember your name with a smile.

6. Don't rush it: Rushing a manuscript into the mail is the mark of an amateur. Take the time to get it right the first time.

7. Shut up and write: The primary difference between the multitudes who say they want to write and the few who actually become working writers is the tenacity to sit down and start typing and keep on typing (OK, "keyboarding") until you have a polished manuscript.

8. Follow your passions: It's said that the test of a professional journalist is the ability to research and write authoritatively about any topic. True enough. But taking it a critical leap farther, what often distinguishes ephemeral "good journalism" from durable *literature* is—passion. Not the moany-groany kind (though it could be that), but rather a heartfelt enthusiasm to thoroughly explore and internalize your topic. The natural world provides my greatest joy and solace in life; consequently, I do my most satisfying and successful work in that realm. Likewise, acknowledge your own passions and follow them courageously.

9. Go back to school: I don't buy the bluff: "I'm a *writer*, not a proofreader; that's what editors are paid to do." Maybe, but getting it right is also what *writers* are paid to do; editors are our safety nets. Writing is communicating, and effective communication requires a fluent command of the basics of composition—grammar, punctuation, spelling and all the boring nuances between. While a tiny few Real Big Names can (sometimes) get away with turning in sloppy work, few do. For the rest of us it's suicidal.

In my years spent warming editors' chairs, I've rejected scores, maybe hundreds of manuscripts for no better reason than mechanical slop—which, I learned straightaway, often suggests mental slop as well. Often, all I needed was a glance at the first page. Most editors feel much the same. If it's worth writing at all, it's worth writing right. To stay sharp, on the cutting edge of marketability, review the basics at least annually. If you can't do it on your own, enroll in a college comp course.

10. Get a life: Fight the urge to become a word-nerd, a literary hermit. Make time to get out and explore new places, meet new people, enjoy (or at least endure) new experiences. Doing so will broaden your literary horizons while investing your words with—not merely verisimilitude, but *life*.

CHAPTER 16

A Nature Writer's Credo

Truth ... for Truth's Sake

In writing, fidelity to fact leads eventually to the poetry of truth.
—Edward Abbey

THIS CHAPTER IS sadly necessitated by the sorry fact that an increasing number of nature writers are openly abusing "literary license" to "enhance" their "nonfiction" with outright lies. By doing so, they're betraying their readers, their editors (who expect nonfiction to *be* nonfiction), nature and themselves. Similarly, by giving themselves the considerable advantage of fabricating scenes and characters at will and presenting them as real, they're cheating the honest majority of writers whose first loyalty is not to "the best possible story," but to lowly truth.

It's gotten so bad of late that even some Heavy Hitters in nature writing not only freely fabricate their "nonfiction," but after winning fame and fortune, brag about having lied in the doing, attempting to justify it as "traditional" and even "necessary," chanting western writer J. Frank Dobie's assertion that he would "never let the truth stand in the way of telling a good story." Stretching this self-justifying concept for laughs, Tom Stoppard allows as how "It is better to be quotable than to be honest," while Mark Twain muses that "Most writers regard the truth as their most valuable possession, and therefore are most economical in its use." Indeed, we live in a dishonest, self-serving, hypocritical culture, the pathology of which has spread even unto nature writing.

Another cliché often associated with this cancer on nonfiction's honor claims that "In order to get at the truth, we sometimes have to lie," which oxymoron, in turn, likely sprang from Picasso's declaration that "Art is not the truth. It is a lie that allows us to approach the truth."

And so on. All of which I refute thusly: That's why God invented fiction. Carter Mackley—publisher of *Bears and Other Top Predators*, a pictorially spectacular quarterly—recently offered this analogy:

> The paintings in this magazine are a product of the artist's imagination. Should the photographs be subject to a different standard? After all, what difference does it make whether there was really a moon behind the wolf, or whether the whales really breached at the same time? The difference lies in story telling. It's the difference between the personal essay and the fictional short story. Truth is stranger than fiction because if a story's not true, it's not so strange—it's just somebody's goofball imagination. But to most of us, it makes a difference if something actually happened. It's more than just a story. It's a true story.

Fiction reflects, and reflects upon, reality. Nonfiction *is* reality; no mere verisimilitude, but the genuine article. Each has its place, fiction and non, and while each necessarily contains elements of the other, nonfiction, to be credible, must substantially deny the temptations of imagination. Which is not to proclaim that nonfiction must ever and always tread an unswerving line of absolute truth, but only and always the heart of the thing. The task of the conscientious nature narrator thus becomes determining—not only for him- or herself, but universally—the ethical limits of creative license in nonfiction. In this contentious, amorphous

and open-ended realm, as it is so often otherwise, I can offer
only opinion.

Morally conscionable narrative devices

Compression and coalescence of events is not merely allow-
able, it's often essential to creative composition—wherein the
writer molds observations, adventures, conversations and
thoughts from various times and places into a single literary
outing. Generally one trip, adventure or event provides the
structural skeleton of the piece, with tidbits pulled from other,
very similar trips, adventures or events to flesh the story out.
To minimize the ethical damage, often as not it's easy to
openly offer some or all of those fleshy bits as just what they
are—recollections: "Last time we were here ..."

Ethical caution: While compression of time and coalescence of events are widely considered credible narrative techniques, their use should be as limited and their presentation
as honest as possible.

Although some may never own up to it, you'd be hard-
pressed to find any established nature writer who has never
compressed and combined in order to create a connected,
meaningful and entertaining narrative: Abbey indulged in
Desert Solitaire, as did Norman Maclean in *A River Runs Through
It* (and then some). Even such icons of the genre as Thoreau
and Petersen are thought occasionally to have dabbled in C&C.
The limit of this particular arm of literary license is, again, *the
heart of the truth:* Everything you claim has happened, must in
fact have happened, just as told.

For example: A chapter in my penultimate book (for marketing majors, that's "the one before this one"), *Heartsblood*,
examines the morality of catch-and-release sport fishing. The
essay is a blend of nature romanticism, angling explication and
eco-polemics, and to provide an active and ongoing example
and carry it along in a pleasant way, I open, occasionally

meander back to touch upon, and close with a composite fishing scene. And so it begins:

> Midsummer. Early evening. The only sounds are a light breeze
> rattling through cottonwoods, the happy twittering of boun-
> tiful birds—melodic robins, raucous jays (three local varieties:
> Steller's, scrub and piñon), the piercing cries of one killdeer,
> the signature *peent-peent* of early-shift nighthawks swooping
> and diving for mosquitoes, the quiescent quacking of a pair of
> greenheads lurking behind a screen of cattails—all overlain
> by the ratchety chatter of my reel as I strip out line and the
> soft wind-whisper of that line arcing out behind me, then
> shooting forward to unfurl and drop, quiet as thought, on the
> water's mirrored face.
>
> Far above, hard-edged platinum clouds laze through a
> sky the color of the South China Sea. Nearer, a great blue
> heron, like some prehistoric memory, approaches for a land-
> ing—wings spread, legs extended—then spots me and flares
> away. Sorry, heron. But I'll stay only the evening, and I'll leave
> all the fish for you.

Setting up a "full-circle" structural approach (discussed earlier, somewhere or another in this growing snarl of pages), I hook a fish and am in the midst of finessing it in—then transition away from the anecdotal intro and into the meat of the essay. Several dozen paragraphs later, having made my points as best I can, I return to the anecdote and bring it home with an exit remark that reflects gently back across the thrust of the polemic and adds a touch of purposeful ambiguity, toward (I hope) a satisfying closure:

> Rushing to the release, I tuck my rod under one arm, reach
> carefully into the water (no net and none needed) and slide
> both palms beneath the temporarily docile animal. While one
> hand gently encircles the tail, the other eases forward to let
> slip the barbless hook. The fish makes no complaint. That

done, I support the brilliant creature upright in open cupped hands, helping it to rest and recover. Seconds pass, then, with one strong torque of tail, the gorgeous salmonid flashes away, diving for the obsidian depths.

Why do we fish—including the many who would never-ever hunt? And what is the morality of our actions?

The answers lie waiting in cold mountain water.

Whether or not this works for you, the point is that I was *not* standing knee-deep in cold mountain water as I mentally masticated the ethical ups and downs of catch-and-release angling, as the structure of the story—meandering between a running anecdote and an involved polemic—at least suggests if never openly implies. *In fact,* I did have a particular piece of water in mind, a particular evening (all those birds) and even a particular fish I'd caught in that particular place on that particular evening. (And yes, in case you wonder, I have seen the South China Sea.) But even had I lacked that single precise memory upon which to base my narrative, I've fished in lots of lakes, heard and seen lots of birds, caught and released lots of fish, thus meeting all the moral requirements for a composite nonfictional narrative.

Disguising identity: It's also, by consensus, "correct" to disguise a real person's identity—perhaps to protect a friend's anonymity, or an enemy's, or merely for creative convenience. Same-same regarding composite characters—just so long as the things your composites say and do are things the real people upon whom they're based in fact have said and done. And here again there are ways to minimize deceit—such as referring to composites pronominally—as "he" or "she"—while eschewing physical descriptions. And often, such a guise can open with some subtle signal of the innocent subterfuge, such as: "Let's just call her …" I like that tack, since it clues alert readers as to what's going on; and so advised, they rarely complain, not even the critics among them.

Selective culling: It's wholly ethical to be ruthlessly selective regarding which bits of a true story you include and which you hack out. In fact, this isn't even "creative license"; it's just writing. As discussed earlier, to work, a story must have a distinguishable beginning, middle and end—but needn't include every inch of the journey.

For example: To achieve the tight, connected, reflective, personal and often lonesome narrative that makes *Desert Solitaire* arguably the finest piece of American nature writing ever committed, Ed Abbey compressed two full summers and several shorter expeditions in Arches National Monument (now Park) into a single "Season in the Wilderness," employing all the techniques just discussed—time compression and coalescence of events, disguising the identities of real people and creating composite characters, creative culling and more. And amongst those things he creatively culled were his second wife and first son, who spent part of one summer with him there. This omission offends some critics and readers (the excised wife and son likely among them) and a certain few literal-minded and/or jealous former fellow monument employees. Yet, for the story to work the way it had to work in order to work at all, Ed had to be alone out there with the sandstone and snakes and lizards and blistering sun. Appropriately, he recalled and seamlessly strung together only those episodes that unfolded when he in fact *was* alone.

No big deal ethically; a very big deal creatively.

Verboten

It's patently unethical to create outright lies and hand them off, actively or passively, as the truth—trips, events, conversations, love affairs, memories, dreams (every time I see "I had a dream …" my B.S. alarm starts screaming), grizzly bears, people, *anything*. Bald-face fabrications have *no* place in narrative nonfiction, "creative" or otherwise.

Likewise, while blending the physical characteristics, thoughts and actions of people you have known is fine for brief scenes and insignificant characters, inventing utterly fictional—detailed, colorful, charismatic—lives, and enlisting them to play major roles in "nonfiction," slops beyond the ethical pale.

There is of course more than one species of truth. When Abbey speaks of "truth" in writing, he's generally referring to *his* writer's credo—a concrete conviction that it's the nonfiction scribe's moral, social and personal responsibility to challenge all the wrongs in the world, most especially those plaguing the writer's own culture. "It's the writer's duty to the good," instructs Ed, "to criticize the bad." It worked for Abbey, and whether it works for you and me or no, we can hardly be true and worthy nature writers without criticizing the bad (say, greed and cancerous growth) in order to defend the good (natural wildness and sustainability). Personally, I love it.

And so, apparently, does gently eloquent poet-farmer Wendell Berry, who opines that "Protest that endures ... is moved by a hope far more modest than that of public success: namely, the hope of preserving qualities in one's own heart and spirit that would be destroyed by acquiescence."

Bravo!

And why *not* protest in print what's wrong with the world? While some won't like it, it's good for all, since, as Walter Lipmann advises: "Where all think alike, nobody thinks much."

My favorite magazine logo—belonging to *Inside/Outside Southwest*—is a stylized X comprising a quill pen crossed with a monkeywrench. Brave words *are* brave acts.

Thoughts on Critics and Criticism

What others say

Criticism is not just a question of taste, but of whose taste. (James Grand)

Book reviewers are little old ladies of both sexes. (John O'Hara)

I am sitting in the smallest room in the house. I have your review in front of me. Soon it will be behind me. (Max Reger)

A critic is a man who knows the way but can't drive the car. (Kenneth Tynan)

Honest criticism is hard to take, particularly from a relative, a friend, an acquaintance or a stranger. (Franklin P. Jones)

Asking a working writer what he thinks about critics is like asking a lamp-post how it feels about dogs. (Christopher Hampton)

I've never yet read a review of one of my own books that I couldn't have written much better myself. (Edward Abbey)

What *I* say

As a blue-collar writer, the only criticism I really care about is book sales.

But of course, that's a damn lie.

Sure I care about what the critics say. And so far at least, they've been more than kind; in fact, compared to my own harsh criticism of my own work, they've been staggeringly generous.

Frustratingly, justifiably bad reviews don't necessarily translate to poor sales (witness many bestselling novels), while great reviews—particularly of lowly "nature books"—rarely precipitate bestsellerdom. Reflecting on this irksome irony, I once remarked to a radio host (off-air) that I'd never likely produce a best-seller because "I'm not that good a writer." Her comeback, quick and kind, was: "*How* you write is not the problem. It's what you write *about* that limits your audience. In this anxious, self-centered, acutely urban world, nature is largely forgotten."

Indeed She is. Why don't more Americans (including Canadians) read more nature writing? And what can we do to reverse this tragic trend?

Poignant, important questions.

But enough of social criticism (for now), and back to the topic at hand: literary criticism, aka "book reviews." As one of English lit's leading figures, the notorious Dr. Johnson, quipped so long ago: "There is nothing more dreadful to an author than neglect, compared with which, reproach, hatred and opposition are names of happiness." That same truism is reflected in the PR cliché: "Even bad ink is good ink."

Certainly, informed, unbiased, intelligent criticism, win or lose, is a godsend. By pointing up weaknesses as well as strengths, constructive feedback can be invaluable to a writer's ongoing self-education; even epiphanous. And while stupid, uninformed and biased reviews are irksome, even those beat utter neglect. Nobody wants to be a nobody. As a fellow writer recently remarked after receiving a chorus of acerbic responses in a magazine letters column, reacting to a politically provocative essay he'd published in the previous issue: "Well, at least I got the bastards' *attention*."

That's the spirit. As Gary Snyder so wisely advises: "It's great not to have had much negative criticism, but there are some people who never have had a negative word said about them, and nobody's read their books either. The point is to enter the dialogue of the times."

Write for your readers and for yourself; forget about the critics.

Miles of Nothing Made or Tainted

Everyone knows that a place exists which is not economically or politically indebted to all the vileness and compromise. That is not obliged to reproduce the system. That is writing. If there is a somewhere else that can escape the infernal repetition, it lies in that direction, where it writes itself, where it dreams, where it invents new worlds. —Helene Cixous

NATURE/WRITING—a double-edged entendre.

To encapsulate and comment one final time on the *craft* of nature writing: If you take nothing else away from this tortuous (not to be confused, I trust, with torturous) tome, I hope it will be a lingering sense of the import and technique of reading as a writer. While our world's cultures and leaders refuse to learn from experience (might spoil their fun), thoughtful writers benefit tremendously from the long history of craft experimentation, win and lose, conducted by those who came (and went) before. How so? By:

- reading and studying what other writers have attempted and
- deciding for ourselves which of those experiments have succeeded, which have failed and why, we can then
- fold those lessons into our own evolving styles and
- forge ahead to create something entirely new and different, maybe even better, in order to
- make our own unique contributions to the ever-expanding horizons of latter-day nature lit.

In sum, it's quite simply bird-brained to start every morning, like a barnyard chicken, from scratch.

Learn to read as a writer, and do so regularly.

Returning now to the *nature* of nature writing—and all my earlier ado about what is and ain't "true nature writing" notwithstanding—I now say: To heck with labels. Just *do it*, any way, any time, anyplace you can.

To quote *Orion's* ever-wise Emerson Blake: "Writing is noble and important, and like it or not, nature writers are agents of cultural change who are leading the way toward a better and saner and more beautiful relationship between humans and our habitats." Just so! If you can manage to insert even one provocative paragraph, one subversive sentence on behalf of nature into everything you write for publication, *that* is nature writing at its best and most useful—more useful in probable fact than a book-length extravaganza of eloquently transcendental musings.

Why? Because "pure" nature writing, as beautiful, meaningful and moving as it can be, tends to be read only by our fellow nature "nuts," putting us in the wheel-spinning position of selling to the sold. Certainly, to expand their knowledge and reinforce and renew their convictions, even the converted need recurring exposure to the inspirational musings of likeminded others; in advertising psychology they call this "decreasing dissonance." Yet, viewed in this oblique light, whole volumes of pure and elegant nature prose are likely of less net value in safeguarding what remains of the natural world and wild-and-free human nature than is *one clean sentence* writ and published beyond the rows of congregational pews, out along the ecotone of marginal interest, out where a few good words stand some chance *of expanding minds and changing lives*. For example:

A commercial hunting magazine is hardly the place you'd expect to find thoughtful, well-crafted, nature-praising prose. And by and large you won't. But then, consider this, by Bill Krenz, writing in a recent issue of *Bowhunter* magazine about a solo pronghorn hunt on the Wyoming plains. As the hunt unfolds, Krenz feels moved to remark that through long experience he's learned that what he wants most from such an adventure is ...

> to see from horizon to horizon. To walk long miles and smell crushed sage in my hands. To flood my senses with antelope country. To bathe myself in the endless blue of a western sky. To taste the dry wind and feel the crunch of sand and gravel under my feet. To sit in the sagebrush and look out over miles and miles of nothing man-made or tainted.

In the arena of craft, this brief excerpt evidences a marked sense for rhythm, parallel structure, and the slow-burning build-up of longing and suspense. The author's descriptions are clear, concise, compelling and, to those of us who've been in such circumstances and felt such stirrings, gratifyingly familiar. In this passage, Krenz truly "takes you there."

But more important than technique—or perhaps we should say, *via* his craft—in this frankly anomalous passage inserted into an otherwise straightforward hunting tale, Krenz kidnaps unsuspecting readers and beams them up to new aesthetic heights of nature-appreciation, promoting the goal of the hunt from narrow *product* to a far broader and more rewarding *process*. At least a few among the many thousands who read that passage—next time they're out there alone, and perhaps for the first time in their lives—suddenly may find themselves emulating the author's joyful appreciation of the broadly diffused gestalt of nature, rather than just one animate, elusive, deliciously edible element thereof.

My belief, my hope, my challenge to you, is that every reader we can introduce—recruit, convert, awaken, expand— to a heartfelt personal appreciation for "miles and miles of nothing man-made or tainted" is one less person who's likely to taint nature and one more who's likely to do what he can to help keep it wild, pure, free and public. Nor does it matter whether such spiritual and ethical edge-dwellers encounter their literary epiphanies in Thoreau's *Walden* or Nelson's *Island* or John Nichols' *Last Beautiful Days of Autumn* or *Bowhunter* or *Orion* magazines or the Sunday section of their local cat-box liner. It matters only that they *do* encounter it, in order that the words, *our* words, can work their metaphorical magic.

Go forth now in joy and confidence, remembering always that peace, beauty, sanity and hope await us ever in nature. By speaking out for the natural world—*our* world—as eloquently, courageously, truthfully and creatively as we can, we are speaking out for life itself, now and forever.

Words, *your* words, can make all the difference in this world.

That said, my bucket is empty.

Time now for a long, slow walk in the woods.

Good luck, comrades.

Selected Bibliography

Abbey, Edward. *A Voice Crying in the Wilderness: Notes from a Secret Journal*. New York: St. Martin's Press, 1989.

——. *Down the River*. New York: E. P. Dutton, 1982.

Baker, John. *The Peregrine*. Moscow, Idaho: University of Idaho Press, 1967.

Byrne, Robert. *1,911 Best Things Anybody Ever Said*. New York: Fawcett Columbine, 1986.

Cahill, Tim. *Jaguars Ripped My Flesh*. New York: Bantam, 1987.

Chicago Manual of Style, 14th ed. University of Chicago Press, 1993.

Cixous, Helen and Catherine Clement. *The Newly Born Woman*. Betty Wing, trans. Minneapolis: University of Minnesota Press, 1986.

Daly, Thomas Aquinas. *Painting Nature's Quiet Places: Conveying Mood and a Sense of Place in Your Paintings*. New York: Watson-Guptill, 1985.

——. *The Art of Thomas Aquinas Daly: The Painting Season*. Arcade, New York: Thomas Aquinas Daly Studio, 1998. (For ordering information, call 800/536-7305.)

de Beauvoir, Simone. *The Ethics of Ambiguity*. Secaucus, NJ: Citadel Press, 1980.

Dillard, Annie. *Living by Fiction*. New York: Harper & Row, 1988.

Gross, John. *The Oxford Book of Aphorisms*. New York: Oxford University Press, 1983.

Guthrie, A. B., Jr. *The Way West*. New York: William Sloane, 1949.

——. *A Field Guide to Writing Fiction*. New York: HarperCollins, 1991.

——. *These Thousand Hills*. New York: Houghton Mifflin, 1956.

Keller, Helen. *The World I Live In*. New York: The Century Company, 1908.

Krenz, Bill. "The Natural Game." In *Bowhunter*, V29 N7.

Langer, Cassandra. "Man and Nature: A Basic Relationship," introduction to *The Art of Thomas Aquinas Daly: The Painting Season*. Arcade, New York, 1998.

Larsen, Michael. *How to Write a Book Proposal*. Cincinnati: Writer's Digest Books, 1985.

Leopold, Aldo. *A Sand County Almanac (with Essays on Conservation from Round River)*. New York: Oxford University Press/Ballantine, 1966.

Levin, Gerald. *Writing and Logic*. New York: Harcourt Brace Jovanovich, 1982.

Levine, Karen. *Keeping Life Simple*. Pownal, VT: Storey Books, 1996.

Little, Brown and Company. *From Manuscript to Printed Book: Exhortations and advice to our authors for preparing manuscripts for the press*. Boston, 1984.

Lueders, Edward, ed. *Writing Natural History: Dialogues with Authors.* Salt Lake City: University of Utah Press, 1989.

Mackley, Carter. Publisher's commentary in *Bears and Other Top Predators,* V2 N1; Spring 2000.

Maclean, Norman. *A River Runs Through It (and Other Stories).* Chicago: University of Chicago Press, 1976.

Murray, John A. *The Sierra Club Nature Writing Handbook: A Creative Guide.* San Francisco: Sierra Club Books, 1995.

Nelson, Richard. *The Island Within.* New York: Vintage/Random House, 1989.

Oxford Dictionary of Quotations, 3rd. Oxford: Oxford University Press, 1979.

Petersen, David. *The Nearby Faraway: A Personal Journey Through the Heart of the West.* Boulder, CO: Johnson Books, 1997.

———. *Elkheart: A Personal Tribute to Wapiti and Their World.* Boulder, CO: Johnson Books, 1998.

———. *Heartsblood: Hunting, Spirituality, and Wildness in America.* Washington, DC: Island Press, 2000.

Petersen, David, editor. *Confessions of a Barbarian: Selections from the Journals of Edward Abbey.* New York: Little Brown, 1991.

Phillips, Larry W., ed. *Ernest Hemingway on Writing.* New York: Touchstone/Simon & Schuster, 1999.

Quinn, Arthur. *Figures of Speech: 60 ways to turn a phrase.* Salt Lake City: Peregrine Smith, 1982.

Shakespeare, William. *The Complete Pelican Shakespeare.* New York: Viking Press, 1969.

Shepard, Florence (Krall). "From the Inside Out—Personal History as Educational Research." In *Educational Theory,* Fall 1988; V38 N4. University of Illinois.

———. "Telling Our Stories, Finding Our Place." Unpublished paper: University of Utah libraries, 1991.

Snyder, Gary. *The Real Work: Interviews & Talks 1964–1979.* New York: New Directions Books, 1980.

Strauss, Susan. *The Passionate Fact: Storytelling in Natural History and Cultural Interpretation.* Golden, CO: North American Press/Fulcrum, 1996.

Strunk, William Jr. and E. B. White. *The Elements of Style* (3rd edition). New York: Macmillan, 1979.

Williams, Terry Tempest. *Leap.* New York: Pantheon, 2000.

———. "Telling It Straight/Risking the Journey." In Florence (Krall) Shepard, "Telling Our Stories, Finding Our Place." Unpublished, University of Utah libraries, 1991.

Writer's Market. Cincinnati: Writer's Digest Books, 1999.

Index